## Praise for *Book Formatting*

*Jennette Green proves that she knows her stuff when it comes to sharing her knowledge and experience in her newest book,* Book Formatting for Self-Publishers, a Comprehensive How-To Guide. *This work is truly a comprehensive guide to formatting for both Print-On-Demand (POD) and ebooks, which covers the most popular venues for those sources.*

*The author combines useful and specific information with clear and simple language to create a handbook for beginners and wanna-bes, as well as being a checklist for experienced writers and self-publishers. What a resource this is! The images of various computer screens as the book progresses makes learning the process even easier.*

— Brenda Jenkins Kleager, MEd

*Efficient, to the point, and easy to follow. It's a concise step-by-step guide that will help you format your own book and have it out on the market in a heartbeat.* Book Formatting for Self-Publishers *is perfect for busy people — from first time authors to small publishing houses — who don't want to spend a lot of time figuring out an instruction manual first. The section on Book Cover preparation was especially helpful, since trying to format that perfect cover can cause many a migraine. Best of all, with Jennette Green's book, you're not only purchasing a very complete instruction book, but you're also receiving the benefit of her years of experience . . . and years of trouble-shooting. This reference book will have a permanent place on my company's bookshelf.*

— Cindy Vincent MAEd, CEO, Mysteriesbyvincent.com
Murder Mystery Party Games & Children's Mystery Party Games
Author, Buckley and Bogey Cat Detective Series, The Daisy Diamond Detective Series

*Excellent book! The topics are organized, detailed, clear and simply put; easy to read. The screen shots are very helpful. The difference in our first book is drastically different from our next one, thanks to reading* Book Formatting for Self-Publishers. *You can really see we followed a professional's example. Even though I was a novice, I was able to turn a basic word document into a professional looking book. Thank you for putting all your hard earned knowledge together for the rest of us. I really appreciate it! This is my reference manual from now on.*

— Janet Lybeck, Author of Teta's Adventures

## Learn How to Achieve Your Publishing Dreams Today!

*Jennette Green's* Book Formatting for Self-Publishers *can help you take control of your publishing career . . .*

Have you written a book that you would like to see published? Today, the barriers preventing an author from getting his/her book published have vanished. No longer do authors need to send out countless query letters to publishers, who either dump them in the trash, or send a standard, cold rejection letter. Now **you** can take control of your publishing career.

In this book, you will learn simple techniques to produce a professional looking print book or ebook. Take advantage of the author's years of experience producing professional book files for satisfied clients. Her tips and tricks to mastering the technical details of publishing a book are presented in a simple, step-by-step format that anyone can understand. Dozens of accompanying illustrations make learning the steps even easier. If you own Microsoft Word and Adobe Acrobat Pro (version 7 or later), you can publish your book now.* With a well-written book, a good marketing plan, and this how-to manual, you can make your publishing dreams come true. What is stopping you? Get started today!

In this book, you will learn how to:

**Use Microsoft Word.** Learn how to format your novel or nonfiction book. Learn tips to make your book look professional.

**Easily Format eBooks.** Use your Microsoft Word print document to create ebooks for Kindle, NOOK, and Smashwords.

**Convert Book Covers.** Discover how to build a book cover on a template. Learn how to convert any book cover file so that it will be accepted at Lightning Source and CreateSpace.

**Apply for Amazon's "Look Inside the Book."** Find out how to format and submit your book to Amazon's "Look Inside" program.

**And much, much more...**

**Jennette Green** is a multi-published, international author of both fiction and nonfiction. She has helped numerous authors and publishers prepare their books for publication. She provides technical support, book and ebook formatting, as well as her specialty of building and converting covers to meet Lightning Source and CreateSpace requirements. Her passion is to empower others to achieve their publishing dreams.

\* Adobe Photoshop (or Scribus) is also needed in order to produce a cover file for Lightning Source.

*If you would like to apply advanced Kindle formatting to your book, please note that this how-to manual does not cover the use of CSS, html, KindleGen, NCX files, or other advanced Kindle formatting issues. If this area is of interest to you, the purchase of a separate book covering these topics is recommended. As well, this manual is best suited for fiction novels, or general nonfiction books. If your print nonfiction book requires a great deal of specialized formatting, you may consider using a professional page layout program, such as Adobe InDesign. The use of InDesign is not covered in this book.*

# Book
# Formatting
## *for*
# Self-Publishers

## a Comprehensive How-To Guide

*Easily Format Books with Microsoft® Word*
*Format eBooks for Kindle, NOOK, Smashwords*
*Convert Book Covers for Lightning Source, CreateSpace*

---

# Jennette Green

DIAMOND PRESS

# Dedication

To all of my friends—you know who you are. Thank you for your encouragement, support, and always...laughter.

# Also by Jennette Green

### Fiction
The Commander's Desire
Her Reluctant Bodyguard
Ice Baron
Murder by Nightmare
(a novelette)

### Nonfiction
*Editor and Co-Author of:*
Lt. Col. John Withers, Civil War Confederate Officer,
In His Own Words
The Civil War through the Eyes of Lt. Col. John
Withers and His Wife, Anita Dwyer Withers

# Table of Contents

# Introduction

ave you written a fiction novel or a nonfiction book that you would like to publish? Would you like your book to be distributed to the major book retailers, such as Amazon and Barnes & Noble? Would you like that book to become available in the popular ebook formats, such as Kindle, NOOK, and Smashwords? You can do it, and it is more simple than you could imagine.

I have spent the last several years formatting and preparing clients' book files for Lightning Source and CreateSpace. All of my clients have been very pleased by the look of their books, and every file was accepted by Lightning Source (LSI), whose rigorous file requirements are well known.

While many people pay book designers (such as myself) to format their books, I'll tell you a secret—it is not hard to turn an ordinary Microsoft® Word® manuscript into a professional looking book. I will show you how easy it is to do, and share the practical tips and tricks I have learned over the years to make the project go smoothly.

This book will give you simple, step-by-step instructions on how to use Microsoft Word 2003 or Microsoft Word 2010 to create a quality, professional looking book, ready for printing with Lightning Source and CreateSpace. In addition, you will learn how to take the Microsoft Word document created for a print book, and turn it into several of the most popular ebook formats. The only software required is Microsoft Word 2003 or Microsoft Word 2010, and Adobe® Acrobat® Professional (version 7 or higher).

You will also learn how to create book covers that will pass the cover standards set by LSI, as well as CreateSpace. Please note that Adobe® Photoshop® is required for LSI covers, as a few of its features are vital in order to adjust the cover images so they meet the 240% ink limits specifications required by LSI. Some publishers use the free online program Scribus for their book covers, but the use of Scribus is not covered in this book.

This book includes many links and references for your convenience. As the internet is a fast-changing environment, please be aware that some links may change.

Are you ready publish your book? Open up your Microsoft Word document, save it under a new name (to preserve your original copy), and let's begin!

*Please note:*  Microsoft Word is best suited for novels or general nonfiction. If you will be publishing specialized nonfiction, with intricate page design, you may wish to consider using a professional page layout program, such as Adobe® InDesign®. The use of Adobe InDesign is not covered in this book.

*1*

# Format a Print Book

## Lightning Source and CreateSpace

irst, a little bit of background. Since you have bought this book, I assume you know that Lightning Source and CreateSpace are the two major players in the Print on Demand (POD) industry. Just for clarification, "Print on Demand" means that a book is printed only when a customer orders it. In this model, publishers do not need to purchase books, or keep inventory piled up in their garages.

CreateSpace is geared toward authors with single titles, and Lightning Source (LSI) is geared toward publishers (or authors starting their own publishing houses) who will publish multiple books. CreateSpace's file requirements are simpler to understand and meet than LSI's. Lightning Source is well known for their complicated requirements for file submissions—especially for cover submissions. But we will get to covers later in this book.

Both LSI and CreateSpace will make your print book available for distribution to major book retailers through their relationship with Ingram. Ingram is a wholesaler/distributor, and Lightning Source is a part of the Ingram Content Group. The main differences between LSI and CreateSpace are the prices they charge for file uploads, proof costs, and the discount you can set for retailers.

By the way, although Ingram makes your book available to major book retailers, such as Barnes & Noble, and your book will be shown as "available" in their online bookstores, getting the retailers to actually stock your book in their "bricks and mortar" stores is another issue entirely.

## Lightning Source

At the time of this book's publication, Lightning Source charges $37.50 each for the interior book block and the cover file, for a total of $75 for each book submission. In addition, they charge $12 per year to include your book in their catalog, which will ensure that your book will be distributed to Barnes & Noble, and will also have access to their worldwide distribution channels.

LSI also offers an option where you can pay $60 so that your book will be included their *Ingram Advance* catalog for one month. Most POD publishers do not choose this option, because books from LSI are placed at the back of the catalog. As far as I know, no POD publisher has yet documented a benefit from paying to be included in the *Ingram Advance* catalog.

Another cost you may pay with LSI includes $30 for a proof of your book. This includes the cost of overnight delivery to you. (CreateSpace print proofs are cheaper.) Also, as of November 2011, LSI now provides free electronic proofs, which can be viewed instead of paying for a print proof to be sent to you. Please visit the following link for more information:

*http://www.ingramcontent.com/MRKNG/2011/52618/52618ClickT hru.html*

It is highly recommended that a publisher view either a print proof, or a free electronic proof, for each book uploaded. If you find errors in your document and would like to submit a new book interior or cover file to LSI, the minimum charge is $40 *per* file. This means that if you want to make changes to both the text and the cover, you will be charged $80. Ouch! Better to get it right the first time. This cost per file applies even if you disapprove the proof and want to make changes to correct issues.

The LSI costs previously mentioned can also be found in LSI's *US POD Agreement*. General information can also be found here:

*http://www1.lightningsource.com/ops/files/pod/USPODOpsManual.
pdf*

Where LSI shines in comparison to CreateSpace is the discount you can set for retailers. For clarification, the term "discount" means the percentage of profit a retailer/wholesaler takes from the book's retail price. The standard discount is 55% of the retail price.

Under the 55% discount model, Ingram, the distributor, takes a 15% discount from the book's retail price for their profit, leaving a 40% discount (profit) for the retailer, which is the minimum retailers require in order to carry the book in their "bricks and mortar" store. This leaves 45% of the book's retail price for the publisher.

However, unless you manage to get your book accepted by Barnes & Noble's small press department, or unless you have an extremely effective marketing campaign, it is unlikely that Barnes & Noble bookstores will carry your book on their shelves. After all, big name publishers vie for space, and often pay hefty prices for end cap displays, and for other featured spots. So, it may not be wise to set a discount of 55% on your book if the major bookstores probably won't carry it in their physical bookstores, anyway.

LSI allows publishers to set the retailer discount as low as 20%. This means that you will receive 80% of the retail price of the book (minus the printing cost for the book). This means more money for you. Another upside of the 20% option is that Amazon will carry your book, and so will Barnes & Noble online, and other online retailers will, too. Even better, customers who visit a "bricks and mortar" Barnes & Noble store can order your book, just like any other book in publication.

By putting more money in your pocket by using the 20% discount model at LSI, you also have the ability to competitively price your book with others in the market. (With the 55% discount, your retail price must be higher, in order to net the same profit as with the 20% discount book.)

Example:

1. A $10 book at 55% discount means that $5.50 goes to Ingram and the retailer, and $4.50 goes to you. Out of this $4.50, you must deduct the cost of printing the book (see the LSI *US POD Ops Manual*, mentioned earlier, for printing prices).
2. A $10 book at 20% discount means $2.00 goes to Ingram and the retailer, and $8.00 goes to you, minus printing costs.

Which sounds better? With the 20% plan you make more money, and, as previously mentioned, you can even lower your price to more closely match your competition from the big name publishers. In addition, if you'd like to sell books to independent stores, you can contact and sell to them directly, and offer them whatever discount you would prefer on your books. Simply order the books from your LSI publisher account at print cost, and ship them directly to your customers. (I'd recommend *not* accepting returns—see why in the note at the end of this section.)

CreateSpace is a different story. If you select their Expanded Distribution Channel (EDC), which provides access to the same distribution network as LSI, (EDC also includes libraries and academic outlets), you must set a discount of 60% for retailers, which means considerably less money in your pocket. What's more, the books are not returnable (a necessity required by retailers), so they will not carry your book in their physical stores anyway—not much different than the 20% model, is it? Except with the 20% model you make more money, and have more control over your price. To make a reasonable profit in the EDC program, you must price your book well above your competition, which is a distinct disadvantage for sales.

*Note:* Although the EDC does not offer returns, many seasoned POD publishers recommend that you do not offer returns with LSI, either. Some publishers have been hit hard with returns a year down the line, after selling a large number of books to a retailer. Their profit turned into a loss.

## CreateSpace

While CreateSpace (CS) may not offer the best discount terms, it does supply other advantages to self-published authors. CS will provide you with a free ISBN, if you do not have your own ISBN, and it is free to set up your files with the "do-it-yourself" option. The "do-it-yourself" option includes distribution to 1) your own Amazon CreateSpace eStore (a 20% retailer discount is required), and 2) the option to distribute to Amazon's website (a 40% retailer discount is required).

However, if you would like to include your book in Create-Space's EDC program, you must pay $25, and, as previously mentioned, a 60% retailer discount is required. In addition, CreateSpace's latest literature for the EDC program states that there is a "$25 book update fee for each new file change request." Please note that this charge applies only to books opted into the Expanded Distribution Channel program.

The file requirements for CreateSpace are not as rigorous as for LSI, and CS offers various do-it-yourself helps and options on its website. Of course, CS also offers a number of book publishing services. CreateSpace is happy to help you with all of your files — for a price. But why pay them, when you can easily do it yourself?

For more information on CreateSpace and LSI, visit the following links:

*Lightning Source:*
*http://www.lightningsource.com*

*CreateSpace:*
*https://www.createspace.com/Products/Book*

For more comprehensive information on the Print on Demand industry, I highly recommend Aaron Shepard's book, *POD for Profit.*

# Microsoft Word 2003 and 2010 vs. Microsoft Word 2007 – the Image Problem

*T*hroughout this book, I will primarily refer to Microsoft Word 2003 and Microsoft Word 2010 when explaining how to format a book for LSI and CreateSpace. Why the exclusion of Microsoft Word 2007? The reason for this is simple— Microsoft Word 2003/2010 software leaves your images alone.

What do I mean by this? Both LSI and CreateSpace require that the images in your file be 300 dpi. (Line drawings should be 600 dpi at LSI.) However, the graphics driver installed in Word 2007 automatically downsamples the image resolution to 220 dpi or less! The Microsoft Word 2003 and 2010 word processing programs do not downsample image resolution. If you want to retain your image quality, you will need to do one of three things:

1. Use Microsoft Word 2003 or 2010. (Not "save as Microsoft Word 2003" in the 2007 version, as the downsampling will still occur.)
2. Use Microsoft Word 2007. It is possible to work around the image quality issue. The best forum I have found on the subject is here:
   *https://www.createspace.com/en/community/thread/15922*
3. Use Microsoft Word 2007, and instead of inserting the images into the document, link to the images within the document. Here is how to do it:

- First turn off Image Compression. In the 2007 version click the Office logo, then *Word Options*. In the 2010 version, go to the *File* tab, and beneath *Help*, click *Options*. Next, for both versions of Microsoft Word, click *Advanced*, and scroll down to "Image Size and Quality." Check the box next to "Do not compress images in the file." (See the image on the next page.)
- Then access the "Link to File" option by going to *Insert*, *Picture*. In the next dialogue box, select the file you would like to insert, and click on the little drop down arrow on the "Insert" button. Select "Link to File" or "Insert and Link." When you need to produce a PDF, *print* to Adobe PDF from the Print menu. Then open your PDF in Adobe Acrobat and check to make sure the resolution of your images have remained 300 dpi, as explained in the section entitled, "Check Image DPI," located on page 95, near the end of *Part One* of this book. While I have never personally tried linking to images in a Microsoft Word 2007 .doc, this is the best information I have gleaned from other professionals in the field. It is certainly worth a try. (See image on next page.)

To be on the safe side, it would be a good idea to turn off the image compression in Microsoft Word 2010, as well. See the preceding instructions to learn how to turn off image compression in both Microsoft Word 2007 and 2010.

Another piece of advice about images in a file: in Microsoft Word 2003, be sure to place the images into the file via the *Insert* menu (*Insert*, *Picture*, "From File"). This method works well for Microsoft Word 2010, too (go to *Insert*, *Picture*, and then click "Insert" to insert the file). Inserting a picture in this manner is an important step for most ebook files, as well.

## *Turn Off Image Compression in Microsoft Word 2010*

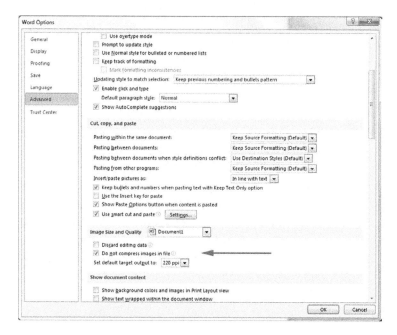

## *Link to Image*

# If Your File has Very Dark (or Light) Black & White Images

*I*f *large* portions of one or more black and white photos in your book are very dark, or alternately, very light, it may be best to adjust the ink percentages a bit in Photoshop before inserting each 300 dpi image into your Microsoft Word document. Otherwise, the very dark areas may print simply as black, with little variation of color, and the light grays may not print as clearly as you would like.

Instead of Photoshop, you could use your favorite image software program to adjust the lighting/contrast of the picture, as well. The output may not be as exact as it would be if the percentages were adjusted in Photoshop, but if you follow the general rule of thumb as written in the following paragraph, it may work out just fine. A tech from LSI stated the following:

> *"I would suggest that they adjust the levels of gray, using the Photoshop 'Levels' and/or the 'Brightness and Contrast' tools, so that the mid-range grays fall between 15% [of 300% ink percentage resolution] for light grays and 85% for darker grays. Anything below 15% may be too light for our press to hold and anything over 85% gray may cause the dot to spread and the ink could appear as black."*

Based upon the tech's recommendation, a good rule of thumb, for images with large sections that are either very light and/or very dark, would be:

1. Light Images: 15% of the maximum allowed 300% ink percentage saturation would equal a minimum ink percentage of 45% for light areas that need to be printed (excluding white, of course).
2. Dark Images: 85% would equal an approximate maximum ink percentage of 255%.

Adobe Photoshop's "Levels" and "Brightness/Contrast" dialogue boxes can be found by going to *Image,* and then *Adjustments.* Some professional photographers recommend using an adjustment layer before making changes to your original photo. More technical information on Photoshop levels can be found if you type "Photoshop Levels" into the Google search engine. In general, you will need to adjust the white and black ends of the histogram spectrum.

While you are adjusting the brightness/contrast or levels of your black and white photo, you can keep an eye on the overall ink percentages of the photo via the *Info* panel. Access the *Info* panel in the Photoshop program by clicking on *Windows,* and then clicking on *Info.* In the *Info* panel's "Panel Options," choose "Total Ink" for the "Second Color Readout." (Make sure that "Actual Color" is selected for the "First Color Readout.")

When you adjust your photo, mouse over the image and note the numbers in the "Total Ink" section of the *Info* panel. Two sets of numbers will appear as you adjust the color. For example, if you mouse over a black area, it might show "300/292." This means that the original color was 300 percent ink saturation, and the new color is 292%.

For more information about determining the ink percentages of your image, go the section entitled, "Check the Ink Percentages in Your Cover Image," which is located on page 170, in *Part Three* of this book.

# Print Preview

$\mathcal{M}$icrosoft Word's *Print Preview* is a wonderful, vital feature that you will consult often when formatting your book. This is especially true after you learn how to designate certain pages in your book to be either odd or even.

When you then pull up *Print Preview* (instructions on how to do this are in the next paragraph), and choose the "Two Pages" option, your book will automatically show up onscreen exactly as it will print in the real book. For example, the even-numbered pages will be on the left side of the screen, and the odd-numbered pages will appear on the right. This visual tool helps tremendously, for you can see immediately if your book pages will print correctly. I absolutely love this feature, and cannot live without it when I format a book.

*Print Preview* can be accessed in Microsoft Word 2003 via two routes: 1*) File, Print Preview* or 2) on the toolbar, click the icon of the magnifying glass hovering over a sheet of paper. Choose the "Two Pages" view.

Print Preview may be accessed in Microsoft Word 2010 by: 1) *File, Print* or 2) "Ctrl + P." Adjust the zoom level in the bottom right corner so that two pages show up on the screen.

> *Note:* In order for *Print Preview* to display odd and even pages correctly, either the "Different odd and even" or the "Mirror Margins" setting must be turned on in the *Page Setup* dialogue box. More on the *Page Setup* dialogue box can be found in the chapter entitled, "Set Up Your Book Trim Size and Margins," on page 18.

# Print View, Normal View and Formatting Code

*S*everal other tools that I automatically turn on when I format a book are either *Normal* or *Print* view, and I always display the *Formatting Marks* within a file.

I find *Print* view to be the easiest to work with when I'm formatting a book, because then I can see what the changes will look like in a medium that looks like an actual book page. However, *Normal* view can be very helpful when dealing with section breaks, as well as when working with a few other specialized details. Some publishers use only *Normal* view. You can determine which view works best for you.

## Display Print or Normal view

1. In Microsoft Word 2003, go to *View,* and then choose either *Print Layout* or *Normal*—whichever works best for you.
2. In Microsoft Word 2010, go to *View,* and then choose either *Print Layout* or *Draft*. Both views can also be accessed by clicking on either the *Print Layout* or *Draft* icon on the Status Bar, which is a horizontal bar located at the bottom of the document window.

## *Normal View in Microsoft Word 2003*

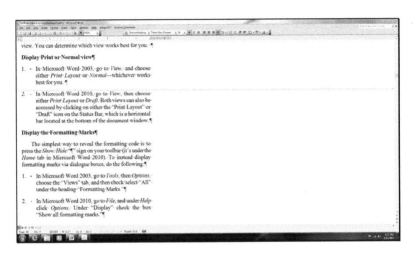

## Display the Formatting Marks

The simplest way to reveal the formatting code is to press the *Show/Hide* "¶" sign on your toolbar (it's under the *Home* tab in Microsoft Word 2010). To instead display formatting marks via dialogue boxes, do the following:

1.  In Microsoft Word 2003, go to *Tools,* then *Options,* choose the "Views" tab, and then check/select "All" under the heading "Formatting Marks."
2.  In Microsoft Word 2010, go to *File,* and under *Help* click *Options.* Under "Display" check the box, "Show all formatting marks."

## Microsoft Word 2003 Dialogue Box

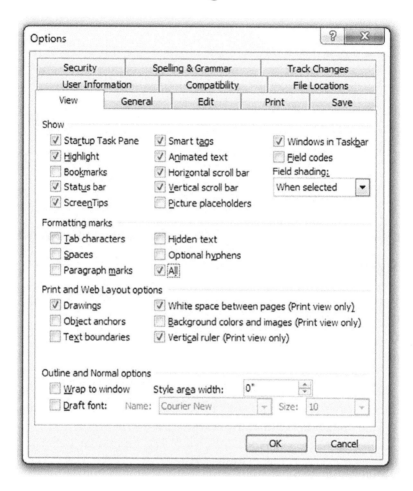

## Microsoft Word 2010 Dialogue Box

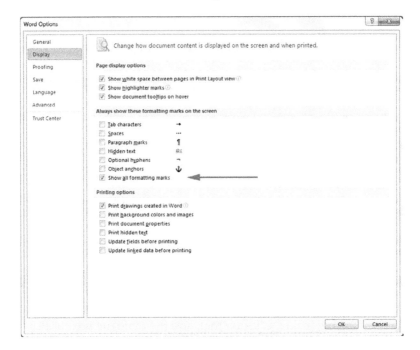

The formatting marks that show up will now reveal all of the paragraphs, tabs, page and section breaks, and various other marks that you will need to see in order to accurately format your book. Viewing the visual "guts" of the code will help tremendously when you apply formatting changes to your document. In addition, this view helps to troubleshoot problems that will arise—and problems will arise. They always do.

# Set Up Your Book Trim Size and Margins

*F*inally, it is time to choose the trim size of your printed book. Will it be 5" x 8", or 5.5" x 8.5", or 6" x 9", or a different size? Whatever the case, now is the time to make your choice.

1. In Microsoft Word 2003, go to *File,* then *Page Setup.*
2. In Microsoft Word 2010, click on the *Page Layout* tab. The bottom portion of that ribbon says *Page Setup.* To the right of the words "Page Setup" is a tiny square box with a little arrow inside. Click on that, and the dialogue box for *Page Setup* will appear.

## Microsoft Word 2010

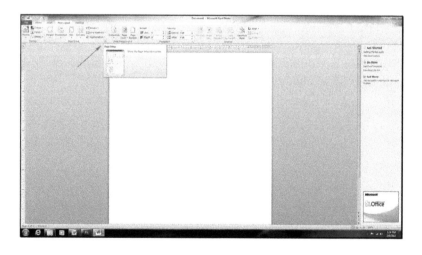

## Enlarged View of Previous Image

As you can imagine, the margins and other page setup attributes will be a little different for each trim size. Since a picture is worth a thousand words, screen shots of each of the dialogue boxes you will need to adjust are included. The dialogue boxes for Microsoft Word 2003 and 2010 are very similar. The images on the following pages are from Microsoft Word 2003.

Just look for the trim size you would like for your book, and copy the settings under each tab. Each of these settings has been used and approved by both clients and this author. However, adjust them as you see fit for your own unique print project.

*Please note:* The margins suggested in the following images are the minimum margin widths I would recommend. If you would like your margins to be a little wider, by all means, make them wider. Measure the margins on several books in your genre which are the same trim size that your book will be. Find a margin width that you like.

No matter what trim size you choose, be sure to select "Apply to Whole Document" in the dialogue boxes, and under the *Margins* tab, be sure to select "Mirror Margins."

*Tip:* I often format books by working on a copy of the original. This leaves the original file untouched. Just use the "save as" function, name it as a new file, and work on the copy. It is also possible to create a new, empty file, apply these *Page Setup* settings, and afterward insert your text. Whatever works best for you is certainly fine.

In order for your odd and even pages to show up correctly in *Print Preview,* and for your left and right headers to work properly, too, click on the "Layout" tab in the *Page Setup* dialogue box. Under the "Headers and footers" section, check the box next to "Different odd and even page." While you're there, check the box next to "Different first page," too. See the following images for additional settings for the *Page Setup* dialogue box.

### *Trim Size 5"x 8" Paper Settings*

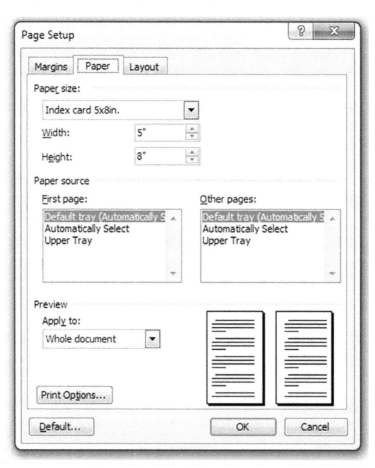

*Trim Size 5"x 8" Margins Settings*

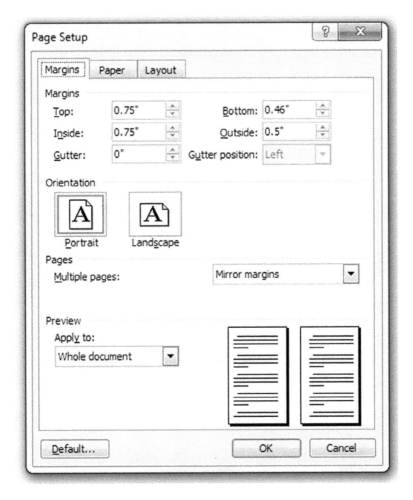

## *Trim Size 5"x 8" Layout Settings*

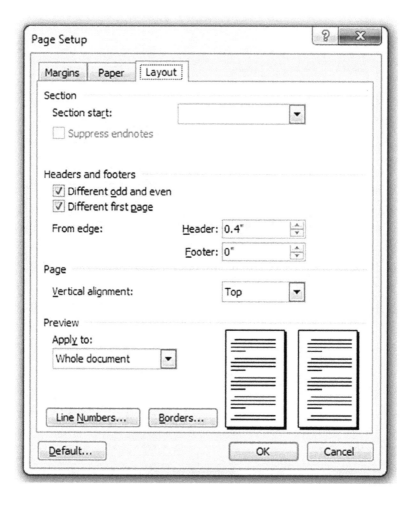

## *Trim Size 5.5"x 8.5" Paper Settings*

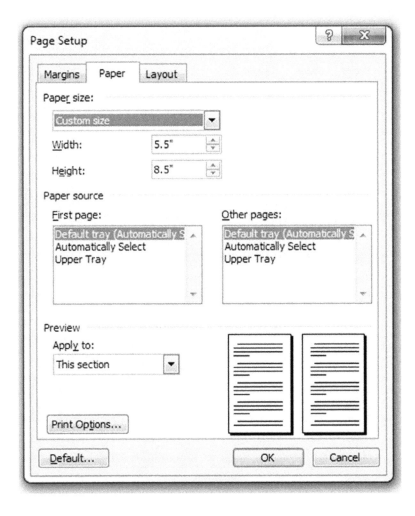

*Trim Size 5.5"x 8.5" Margins Settings*

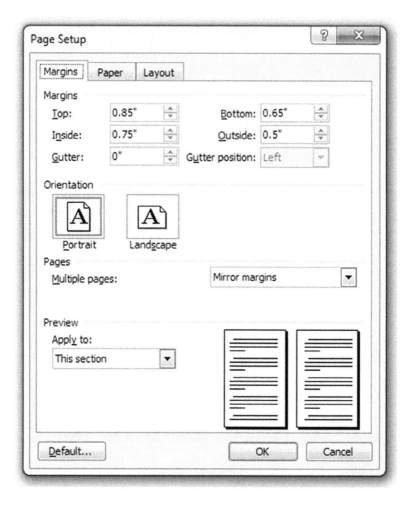

*Trim Size 5.5"x 8.5" Layout Settings*

*Trim Size 6"x 9" Paper Settings*

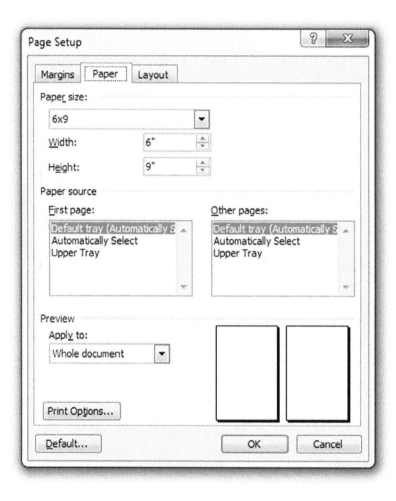

*Trim Size 6"x 9" Margins Settings*

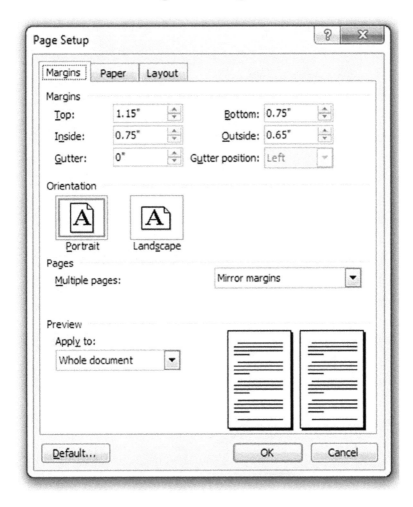

*Trim Size 6"x 9" Layout Settings*

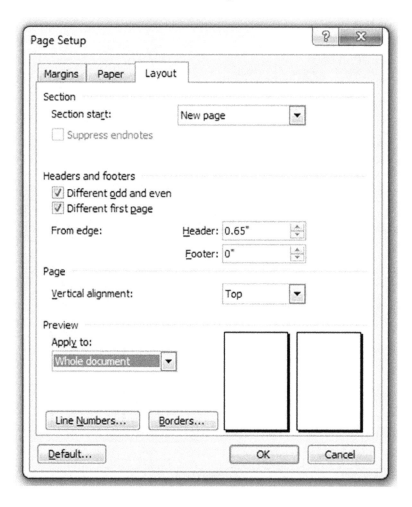

# Consistency of Style

One of the keys to achieving a professional looking book is to maintain consistency of style throughout your manuscript. This means that the measurement of the indents at the beginning of each paragraph must be the same throughout the book. All chapter title headings should be formatted in the same font, and placed exactly the same distance from the top margin in every chapter. In addition, the opening text of the first page of each chapter should begin exactly the same distance from the top margin in every chapter. Even the number of spaces at the end of each sentence matters. We will address each of these issues a little later.

For now, here are a few basic rules to follow when formatting any book:

1.  Do not overuse bold, italics, or ALL CAPs. It makes the output look cluttered, busy, and worst of all, amateurish. Underlining is not typically used in print books.
2.  Use curly quotes (Palatino Linotype quotes: " " or ' ', or Times New Roman quotes: " " or ' '), not straight quotes (" " or ' ').
3.  Use one font (also known as a typeface) for your body text, and perhaps a different typeface for your titles, chapter titles, and headers. This generally means a maximum of two to three different fonts in your book. If you look through any professionally published book, the number of typefaces used is minimal. Too many fonts makes a book look cluttered and amateurish. This goes for the cover, as well.
4.  Use serif fonts (serifs are the little "feet" at the bottom of the letter stems), such as Times New Roman, Garamond, or

Georgia, for body text. Serifs help the eye flow to the next letter. Many people find serif fonts much easier to read for prolonged periods of time, which is why virtually every professionally published book uses a serif font for their body text.

5.   Sans-serif fonts (fonts with no serifs), such as Arial or Franklin Gothic Book, are generally used for chapter titles or text that is set apart, such as in a tip box. A change in font helps a reader see at a glance that certain parts of a page are different, and require special attention.

6.   Use "em" dashes (—) instead of two dashes (--) throughout your book.

7.   Use an "en" dash (–) to separate a range of items, such as "pages 11–27" or "May–June."

# Set Up Body Text Format Style

*I*n this chapter, we'll be making changes to the body text with a view to future tasks—namely, converting your book to the various ebook formats. If you get the formatting right now, your task of making the ebooks later will be much easier. While some of these steps may not be necessary if you do not plan to convert your manuscript into ebook format, they will still ensure a consistent, professional looking book manuscript now.

First, *select all of your text from the Chapter One title heading all the way to the end of your manuscript.* The easiest way to do this is to click your mouse at the beginning point of the Chapter One heading, and then press the three keys "Ctrl + Shift + End." The entire document (from Chapter One to the end) will now be highlighted.

Now it is time to format the paragraphs in your document. Here's how:

1. In Microsoft Word 2003, go to *Format,* then *Paragraph.*
2. In Microsoft Word 2010, go to the *Page Layout* tab, and look for the *Paragraph* section. (The word "Paragraph" will be on the bottom edge of the ribbon, just like "Page Setup" was in the previous section.) Click the tiny box with the arrow in it, just to the right of *Paragraph,* and a dialogue box will appear. Again, the dialogue box in both versions of Microsoft Word is very similar.

Under "Indents and Spacing," choose the settings "Alignment: Justified" and "Outline level: Body Text." Under "Special" choose "First Line" and then the amount you would like your first line to be indented. In the next image, 0.33" is selected for first line indents, but

0.25″ or 0.3″ will do just as well. Choose whatever you think looks best in your manuscript. Last of all, under "Line spacing" choose "Single." This last step is important if you plan to format the document into an ebook later. (If your print document requires exact spacing, then do not apply this step until you are ready to format your ebook in a separate document.)

> *Please note:* Applying the "First Line" indent to your document means that any numbered or bulleted lists will also be indented. So will chapter titles, and perhaps other specialized formatting in your book. You will learn how to fix these extra indents in the chapter entitled, "Format Chapter Title Headings," on page 55. While applying the "First Line" indent may cause a few problems to be fixed later, it ensures consistent paragraph indentation throughout your document. As well, for ebook formats such as Smashwords, it helps to reduce potential conversion problems if you apply the same style to the whole document.

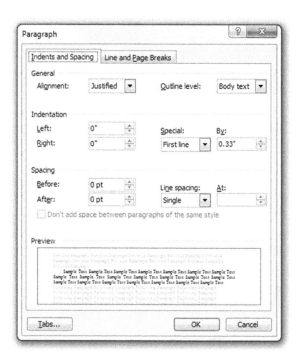

Under the "Line and Page Breaks" tab, be sure to check the "Widow/Orphan" box, so that a single line of text will not be "orphaned" at the top of any page in your manuscript.

*Note:* Some major publishers allow widows and orphans in their books. For example, the hardcover J.K. Rowling books occasionally allow one line of text to be printed at the bottom of one page, with the remainder of the paragraph following on the next page. These books do not, however, allow a single line of text to be printed alone at the top of the page (unless it is a one line paragraph). Other publishers allow widows and orphans on both pages. The choice is up to you, although most design books recommend eliminating all widows and orphans.

## Refine Justification

This next tip was gleaned from Aaron Shepard's wonderful book, *Perfect Pages*. He discovered that the default justification system for the Microsoft Word program is rather "loose." It only has the ability to adjust the spaces between words, which "stretches" the space, rather than "squeezes" it. Usually this ends up looking fine. However, it *is* possible to turn on an option that will enable Microsoft Word to both "squeeze" and "stretch" the space between words. It can be found here:

1. In Microsoft Word 2003, go to *Tools, Options,* and then go to the "Compatibility" tab. Check the box next to "Do full justification like WordPerfect 6.x for Windows" and click *OK.* (Do not adjust any of the other boxes—leave them in their default settings.)

2. In Microsoft Word 2010, go to the *File* tab. Under *Help* click on *Options.* In the next dialogue box click on *Advanced,* and then go to the very bottom where it says "Layout Options." Click on the little down arrow next to it, and scroll down and check the box next to "Do full justification the way WordPerfect 6.x for Windows does." (Do not adjust any of the other boxes—leave them in their default settings.)

## *Microsoft Word 2003*

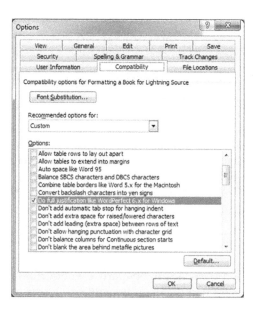

## Microsoft Word 2010

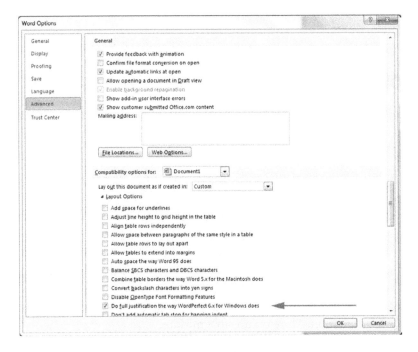

Sometimes this setting squeezes words too close together, so that it looks like two words are mistakenly run together into one. I've found that this doesn't happen as much if hyphenation is turned on (see the next section). However, when you've finished formatting your book, it would be a good idea to check for spacing irregularities when you do the final proofing of your manuscript (before converting it to PDF).

*Tip:* Sometimes, when a paragraph is justified, the last sentence—even if only two or three words—will unnaturally s-t-r-e-t-c-h to the end of the line. This can be eliminated by adding a paragraph return to the end of the line.

# Hyphenation

nother important step you can take to improve the look of your justified text is to turn on Microsoft Word's automatic hyphenation. Please note that this step is not required—some publishers prefer to hyphenate, and some do not. If you would like to add hyphenation to your book, read on.

Hyphenation can smooth out the spaces between words, and make the document's text look more evenly distributed on the page. However, please note that adding hyphenation to your book also means that you must carefully look over your document after adding the hyphenation. More on this in a minute.

1. In Microsoft Word 2003, go to *Tools, Language, Hyphenation*.
2. In Microsoft Word 2010, go to the *Page Layout* tab, and click the little down arrow next to Hyphenation. Choose "Hyphenation Options."

You will not want short words hyphenated. Neither will you want multiple hyphenations in a single paragraph. You can control this by checking the box "Automatically hyphenate document," (I prefer to uncheck the "Hyphenate words in CAPS), enter "0.5" for the "hyphenation zone," and "Limit consecutive hyphens" to 1 or 2. See the following image.

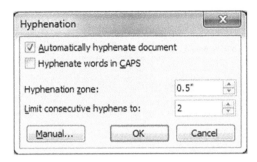

While hyphenation can make your text look tighter, and more professionally typeset, it can also cause problems. For example, you will not want a word hyphenated between two pages (one half of a word on one page and the other half on the next page). In addition, you may not want certain words hyphenated.

*Tip:* If hyphenation is turned on, I always go through the final document, one page at a time, to make sure that everything looks like it should before I convert it to the final PDF for printing.

## Eliminate Hyphenation in a Paragraph

When you find a word that you do not want hyphenated, you have several options available to correct the issue. This first method will eliminate hyphenation from the entire paragraph.

1. In Microsoft Word 2003, go to *Format, Paragraph.*
2. In Microsoft Word 2010, go to the *Home* tab, and click the little down arrow next to *Paragraph.*

Simply check the box entitled, "Don't hyphenate." This setting will affect only that paragraph.

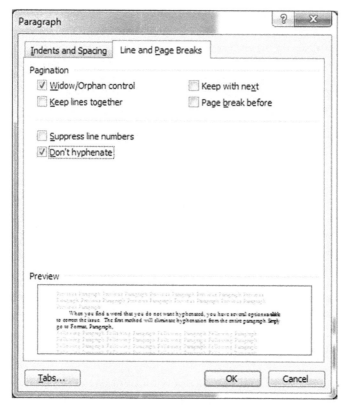

## Eliminate Hyphenation in a Word

The second method eliminates hyphenation from only one word in the paragraph. In Microsoft Word 2003, select the entire word (be certain it is spelled correctly first), then go to *Tools, Language, Set Language,* and check the box entitled, "Do not check spelling or grammar," and click *OK.*

I have been unable to find this feature in Microsoft Word 2010. With Microsoft Word 2010, instead simply follow the instructions for "Eliminate Hyphenation in a Paragraph."

## Adding an Optional Hyphen

It is possible to insert an Optional Hyphen (manually insert a hyphen) into your document. This can be achieved by using the "Control" and "-" keys. I don't recommend this, for one reason only; it may show up in your ebook, too. These hyphens are often referred to as "ghost" or "soft" hyphens. (This problem may also occur if you use Microsoft Word's manual hyphenation option.) Since the text in ebooks flows differently on eReader devices than on a printed page, that means the hyphenated word may show up in the middle of a sentence! Now that would look unprofessional.

If you absolutely must insert a hyphen (or another character spacing adjustment, such as adding spaces to a paragraph, kerning characters, etc.) into your document, keep careful note of each change. When you format your ebook, you will need to go back and delete those settings.

## Insert Non-Breaking Space or Hyphen

Sometimes you may have the initials of a name, or a word followed by ellipses that you do not want split between two lines. An example might be "Well. . . ." If this word and the ellipses were placed at the end of a line, a few of the ellipses might print on one line, with the remainder on the next line. That would not look right at all. To prevent this from happening, insert a non-breaking space. On the keyboard, press "Ctrl + Shift + Space" in the location where you would like the non-breaking space to be.

At other times you may have letters or numbers separated by a hyphen, but you do not want them split onto separate lines. An example of this might be a part number, such as "Model T-11." To prevent the part number from hyphenating, insert a non-breaking hyphen. On the keyboard, press "Ctrl + Shift + Hyphen."

# Find and Replace

ertain invisible characters in the manuscript can cause trouble, especially when converting your document to ebook formats. Among these troublesome characters are tabs, manual line breaks, and spaces. When the formatting marks are displayed (Show/Hide), tabs look like an arrow pointing right (→). Manual line breaks look like an arrow pointing down, then pointing left (↵). It is best to get rid of them now. Make sure that you have turned on the formatting marks, as described earlier.

For each *Find and Replace* function recommended here, you may find it beneficial to go through your document and replace each instance individually. Then you will not have any unpleasant surprises, as you might if you instead did a "blanket" Replace All.

*Find and Replace* can be found:

1. In Microsoft Word 2003, go to *Edit,* and click on *Replace.*
2. In Microsoft Word 2010, go to the *Home* tab, and in the *Editing* section, click *Replace.*

## Find and Replace Manual Line Breaks

To delete the manual line breaks, place "^11" (without quotes) in the *Find* box, and "^p" (for a paragraph ¶ symbol) in the *Replace* box. This will replace the manual line break with a standard paragraph return. I always replace these individually, to make sure that an extra paragraph symbol is only inserted where needed.

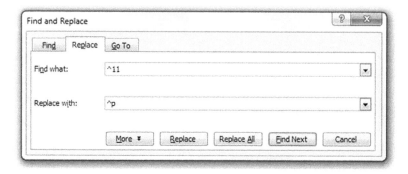

## Find and Replace Tabs

Tabs inserted at the beginning of each paragraph in your manuscript can cause problems later, when you want to convert it to an ebook. In a prior step, we took care of the paragraph indent requirement by creating the "first line indent." Now we can delete those unnecessary tabs. Again, you may want to go through your manuscript and individually replace tabs, just to make sure no unwelcome surprises greet you when you go through your manuscript later. To delete the tabs, place "^t" in the *Find* box, and put nothing in the *Replace* box.

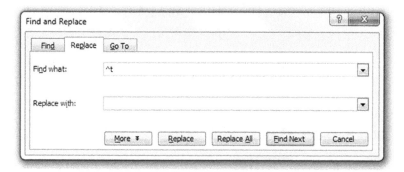

Perhaps you used tabs to create a block of indented text. It is always best to delete all of these tabs, and then select the paragraph and format it by going to *Format, Paragraph* (*Home, Paragraph* in 2010), and choosing the right and/or left indentation under the *Indents and Spacing* tab. An example is listed in the next image.

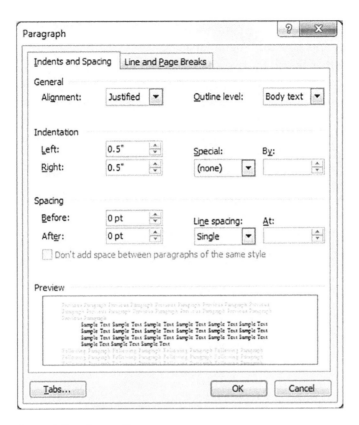

## Find and Replace Spaces

Rogue spaces can create havoc in a manuscript. Publishers generally follow the end of sentence period (.) with one space, and then start the next sentence. If you would like to do the same, under the *Find* tab type two spaces. In the *Replace* box, type one space. Replace all.

What do I mean by "rogue" spaces? Well, sometimes authors indent paragraphs by using the space bar. Spaces are not uniform, and it is virtually impossible to create consistent indentation by using spaces. First line indents, as mentioned earlier, are a much better method.

Other examples of "rogue" spaces are ones that show up in the middle of the manuscript—perhaps in the middle of a paragraph! This happened with one project I recently completed. I hadn't spotted the extra spacing in the Microsoft Word .doc, so it ended up creating a very odd looking paragraph in the PDF file. I always check my manuscripts now for "rogue" spacing.

Do another search for two spaces. This time, only use the *Find* box. Go through the document and look for "rogue" spacing. (If you chose to keep two spaces after a period (.), instead look for three spaces now.) Fix any problems you find. You will be glad you did!

A handy list of special character symbols used for "find and re-place" in Microsoft Word can be found at the following links:

*http://office.microsoft.com/en-us/word-help/find-and-replace-text-or-other-items-HA001230392.aspx*

*http://support.microsoft.com/kb/214204*

# Section Breaks

*Y*ou are much closer to finishing the formatting of your book. The only items remaining are 1) separating your book into sections, 2) formatting chapter title headings, 3) applying headers and page numbers, and then 4) saving your book in the PDF/X-1a:2001 file format required by Lightning Source and CreateSpace.

Before continuing, click on the *Print Preview* button ("Ctrl + P" in Microsoft Word 2010) and take a good look through your book to make sure that the main body text of your manuscript looks like it should. If there are any problems, now is the time to fix them. (*Note:* Do not worry about chapter title headings at this time. Those will be formatted in the next chapter.)

When you applied the formatting to the body text, remember that you only applied the first line indents from Chapter One to the end of the book. The beginning of your book—the title page, copyright page, etc.—were not selected on purpose. You do not want line indents in those sections, otherwise the title centering will be thrown off. If, however, you discover that the titles *are* indented, select those sections and move the indent tab to the left margin. You can also fix "numbered list" indents in the same manner. See the chapter entitled, "Format Chapter Title Headings," on page 55, for more information.

## Book Layout

You probably have a good idea of how you would like the front matter of your book to look. Typical scenarios might include:

1. Title page (on right side/odd page)
2. Copyright page (on left side/even page)
3. Dedication (usually on right side/odd page)
4. Table of Contents (on right side/odd page)
5. Chapter One (on right side/odd page) (For formatting purposes, I include the first page of Chapter One as part of the "front matter" in this book.)
6. If you have any "Parts" in your book (such as Part One, Part Two, etc.), those will be on the right side/odd page, as well. The first chapter immediately following the new "Part" should also be on the next right/odd page.

Each page of the front matter must be separated by a section break. When you previously set up the book's page layout by using the *Paragraph* dialogue box, you checked the boxes for "different first page" and "different odd and even page."

By making each page of the front matter a separate section, Microsoft Word sees each page as a "first page." This means that headers will not be applied to these pages, unless you specifically put a header on those pages. This is a handy tool, because you do not want headers on the title page, copyright page, etc. And you certainly do not want headers on the first page of each new chapter. Just look at any professionally published book, and you will see what I mean.

When a book is printed, you will want certain pages to print on a specific type of page—either odd or even. Now is the time to tell Microsoft Word how to make your document behave so it will print properly.

Make sure that your document is in Normal (Draft) view, with the formatting marks (Show/Hide) turned on.

In the following two sections, you will learn that you can use either "odd page" and "even page" breaks, or you can use "next page" breaks to separate your book into sections. Either will work. Choose the method that seems simplest and that will work best for you. Read both sections, however, for some of the information contained in the "Odd and Even Section Breaks" will pertain to the "Next Page Section Breaks," too.

### Odd and Even Section Breaks

You will want your title page to be on an odd page. One way to achieve this is to go to the bottom of the page and choose:

1.  In Microsoft Word 2003 go to *Insert,* then *Break,* then under "Section break types" choose "Even page." This will ensure that the next page is an even page.
2.  In Microsoft Word 2010 go to the *Page Layout* tab, and in the *Page Setup* section, click *Breaks,* and choose "Even Page.") This will ensure that your *next* page will be delineated as an even page.

## *Microsoft Word 2003*

## *Microsoft Word 2010*
### *Breaks panel is enlarged*

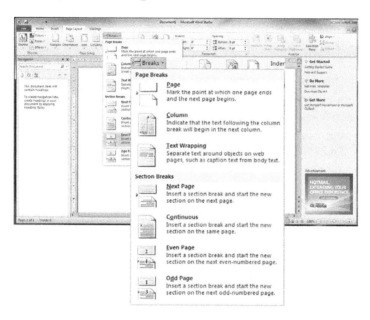

## *Example of Even Page Break on Title Page*

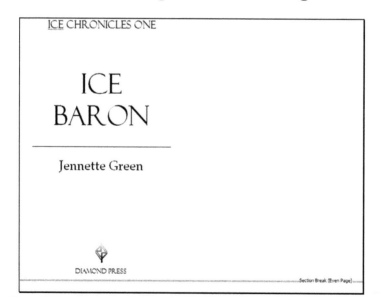

At the end of the next page (perhaps the Copyright page), you would insert an "Odd page" section break. And so on. This is especially helpful when your last page before Chapter One ends on an odd page, and you want your first chapter to begin on an odd page. Just insert an "odd page" break at the end of that last, odd page, and Chapter One will automatically begin on the next odd page. There is no need to insert a blank page in the document when you use "odd" and "even" page breaks.

### Next Page Section Breaks

Although I prefer to insert "odd page" breaks and "even page" breaks, "next page" breaks work equally well for the front matter pages, and to separate chapters in the book. In addition, I am sure they are less confusing. However, if you use "next page" breaks, you will need to be certain to add extra, blank pages where required, so that your front matter book pages will print on the correct (odd/even) pages. Just use additional "next page" breaks as needed.

If you need to insert two consecutive "next page" breaks in your manuscript, do not separate them with a number of paragraph returns. One extra paragraph return between the breaks is all that is needed.

### Check Your Section Breaks in Print Preview

Look at your book in *Print Preview*. The title page should be alone on the page, with a space to the left. The other pages will show up exactly as they will be printed. Does your book look the way you want it to print? Does the title page need centering? Does the text for the copyright page fit on one page?

The following are images of the first seven pages of one of the books published by Diamond Press. You will note that this book started with an excerpt from the book. However, the title page could easily be placed on the first page, instead.

The next two pages show how a book (in general) should look in *Print Preview*.

*Pitch black had settled in outside.* With it, a deep, biting cold swirled into the cave.

She really should put out the fire.

But it was so warm and friendly. And Anya felt so alone.

*Put it out.* It was time to get going. Although the cave entrance was partially blocked, someone at the perfect angle might see the light. Maybe that one, last, persistent pilot—although she hadn't heard the craft since noon. He must have given up, too. For now.

Unfolding her trowel, Anya chipped up a mound of frozen ice and mud and cast it onto the fire. It flickered, but didn't go out.

"Don't put it out on my account."

The low, rough voice made her gasp, and she whipped out her laser.

*Joshua.*

He seemed to fill the entrance. The elite, cream military parka made his shoulders seem wider, his body more solid and forbidding.

"You." Hands trembling, she lowered the weapon.

"Of course it's me. I'm your protector, foolish girl. Who did you think would come for you?"

Palpable fury simmered in him, deep and hot, yet tightly leashed, as were every one of his emotions, always. In the past, she had wished that just once she could break through the impenetrable shell he enclosed around himself. Just once, she'd like to see him snap, to glimpse the true man underneath all the medals and the power that fit him like a glove. To especially see beyond the shiny honor of hero worship with which she'd clothed him when they had first met. She had always wanted to please him.

No more.

Also by Jennette Green

The Commander's Desire
Her Reluctant Bodyguard
Murder by Nightmare
*(a novelette)*

ICE CHRONICLES ONE

# ICE BARON

Jennette Green

DIAMOND PRESS

ICE BARON

A Diamond Press book / published in arrangement with the author

Scripture quotation taken from the New American Standard Bible®.
Copyright © 1960, 1962, 1963, 1968, 1971, 1972, 1973,
1975, 1977, 1995 by The Lockman Foundation.
Used by permission. (www.Lockman.org)

ISBN: 978-0-9844044-4-3

Library of Congress Control Number: 2011931402
Library of Congress Subject Headings:
Love stories
Romance fiction
Futuristic romance
Science fiction
Man-woman relationships—Fiction

Diamond Press
3400 Pegasus Drive
P.O. Box 80043
Bakersfield CA 93380-0043
www.diamondpresspublishing.com

Published in the United States of America.

*"Have I not commanded you?*
*Be strong and courageous!*
*Do not tremble or be dismayed,*
*for the LORD your God is with you wherever you go."*

*JOSHUA 1:9* NASB

## PROLOGUE

*Former Kazakhstan*
*Astana, Donetsk Territory, year 3145 A.D.*
*(Millennial Ice Age, caused by Nuclear holocaust)*

ANYA PRESSED HER FOREHEAD to the cool, curved window of the school library and looked down at the earth, a kilometer below. She felt safe here, although she was no longer a child. Unfortunately, the feeling of peace was an illusion. Soon her protector, the current Baron of Donetsk Territory, would find her and she would have to face her future.

If only she could escape. If only she could ride down the slender metal umbilical cord elevator which anchored the sky city of Astana to earth, and flee what was coming.

The glass felt cool against her skin, and the room behind her lay silent, as it was nearly time for supper. Quiet, too, was the vast wasteland of ice and snow which stretched out as far as her eyes could see—land that had been ruled by her family, the Dubrovnyks, until her father had died ten years ago. The frosty view remained the same all year round. Spring and summer were too cold to melt the snow. On a clear day, she could see the great Tien Shan mountain range far to the south. Her uncle lived south of the Tien Shan, and her territory had been engaged in a bloody war with his for her entire life. To the east, Donetsk Territory fought a different, but equally vicious war with Altai Territory. Altai's leader, Onrod, was Astana's special guest this weekend.

"Anya." Joshua's deep, quiet voice startled her.

Note that in the previous images, headers are not present on any of the front matter pages.

To prevent headers from printing on the first page of the chapters following Chapter One, you will need to insert a "next page" break at the end of each chapter. Do that now.

## Eliminate Extra Paragraph Returns

This is a good time to eliminate any extra paragraph returns that may exist in your manuscript. It is likely that most of them immediately precede the section breaks you just put into your manuscript.

I recommend no more than one or two paragraph returns before a section break. (Sometimes you will want none at all.) Otherwise, the invisible paragraph returns might tell the Microsoft Word program to add an extra, blank page where no blank page is needed. Minimizing the number of paragraph returns in a document is an important step for preparing your book to be converted into an ebook later, too.

Check through each section of your manuscript, including the front matter pages.

*Hint: Never, never, never separate pages or chapters by using paragraph returns! This will foul up your formatting every time.*

### *Too Many Paragraph Returns at End of Chapter*

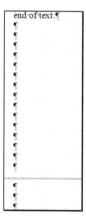

## *Good Number of Paragraph Returns at End of Chapter*

```
end·of·text.¶
  ¶
..................................................................
  ¶
  ¶
  ¶
```

Turn on *Print Preview* (two page view) and quickly go through your document to make sure that your book pages will print on the correct pages.

The title page of your document should show up on right side, with no page to the left. If you scroll down, the copyright page should be on the left, dedication on the right, and Chapter One on the right, just as depicted in the previous images.

> *Note:* Chapters Two and later may be printed on either an odd or an even page. That is why a "next" page break is inserted at the end of each chapter. As a result, the following chapter will automatically begin on the next page.

Make certain your chapter title heading is present on the first page of each chapter. If not, now is the time to fix that problem. (We will format the chapter title headings and delete extra indents in the next chapter.)

Sometimes you will discover that you have made a mistake, and you will need to change an "odd page" break into an "even page" or "next page" break. At times, Microsoft Word will confound your attempts to delete the old break and insert the new one. More than once I have deleted an "odd page" break, inserted a "next page" break, and then gone to *Print Preview*, and it still "prints" as an odd page. When I go back to normal view and look at the section break formatting code, the code has switched back to the original "odd page" break! Where did the "next page" break go? What can be done in this situation?

A simple enough solution (although cumbersome and quite annoying), is to insert two "next page" breaks (be sure to separate each page break with a paragraph return) before the "odd page" break, and two more "next page" breaks after the "odd page" break, for a total of five page breaks. Then select the first four page breaks (two "next," the "odd," and a "next"), and delete them, leaving only one "next page" break. Now check print preview and see if the problem is fixed. Usually that does the trick.

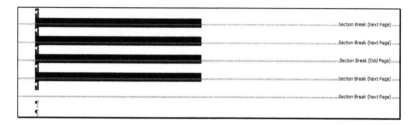

Of course, using *only* "next page" section breaks, instead of "odd" or "even" section breaks, would eliminate the problem, as well! Another point in favor of using only "next page" section breaks.

# Format Chapter Title Headings

*A*t this point, the body text in your book should be format-ted correctly, and indented using the first line indent function that was described earlier. Unfortunately, when this function was applied from Chapter One through the end, all of the text, including the chapter title headings, was indented. Now is the time to get rid of the indents for the chapter title headings. (If you have additional headings, numbered lists, blocks of indented text, etc., in your manuscript, you will need to reformat those areas, as well. After you have formatted your chapter title headings, be sure to go back and do so.)

Open the *Styles and Formatting* panel:

1.  In Microsoft Word 2003, go to *Format,* then *Styles and For-matting*.
2.  In Microsoft Word 2010, you can access the *Styles* panel two ways. 1) press "Alt +Ctrl +Shift + S," or 2) go to the *Home* tab, and click little down arrow next to *Styles*.

Now, using your mouse, select/highlight the text for your Chap-ter One heading. Adjust it, if necessary, so it is the font and size you would like. Now, go to the top ruler. Notice the little triangular button that is pointing downward. It is indented almost three clicks from the left margin.

## Enlarged View of Previous Image

Click on it and drag it left, so that it is flush with the left margin, like the following picture:

## Enlarged View of Previous Image

By the way, this setting will only apply to the text that is high-lighted.

Once you have formatted your chapter title heading to your liking, keep the chapter heading highlighted and look over in the *Styles and Formatting* box on the right side of your screen. In Microsoft Word 2003, the box at the very top is the style that has been assigned to your chapter heading style. In Microsoft Word 2010 a blue box outlines the selected style.

Usually, the name of the style is generic gibberish, such as "16 pt, Centered," as depicted in the next image. To name the style something that you can easily remember and find again, rename it. Right click on the box and choose "Modify Style..."

## *Microsoft Word 2003 Styles and Formatting*
*Styles and Formatting panel section is enlarged below. I right-clicked on the style in order to bring up the "Modify Style" option.*

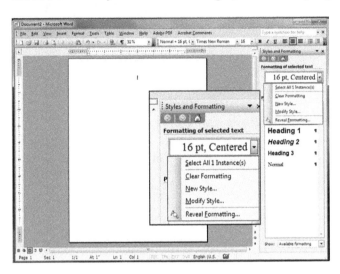

## *Microsoft Word 2010 Styles*

In the next dialogue box, you will see the "gibberish" title that Microsoft Word gave your chapter heading style.

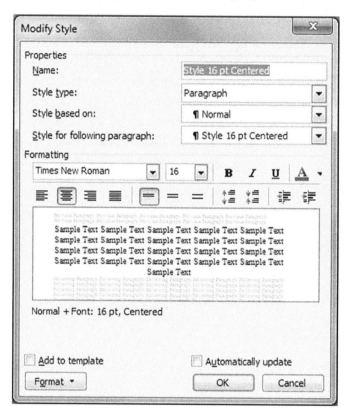

Here is your chance to change it into something you will re-member. In the highlighted box, type (without quotes) "Chapter-Heading." Now, it will show up in the *Styles and Formatting* panel named as "ChapterHeading." Whenever you want to apply the ChapterHeading style to other chapter headings, you need only select the text to which you would like to apply that style, and then click "ChapterHeading" in the *Styles and Formatting* panel.

If you do not want your chapter title headings to hyphenate, use this same "Modify Style" dialogue box to set that parameter. Within the box, click *Format*, and then *Paragraph*. Under the "Line and Page Breaks" tab, check the box entitled, "Don't hyphenate."

Go through your document and format your chapter headings with your new style.

The beauty of *Styles and Formatting* is three-fold. First of all, the style of your chapter title headings will remain consistent throughout your manuscript.

Second, if you want to change the style of your chapter headings, all you will need to do is:

1. Select all instances of the style in your document. You can do this by right clicking on the style heading, as shown in the first image on page 57. Click "Select All # Instance(s)."

2. Then right click the style again, and modify your "ChapterHeading" style. The updates will automatically be made to all of the chapter headings in your manuscript which are highlighted.

Third, if you would like to insert a Table of Contents in the beginning of your manuscript, you can choose "ChapterHeading" as your number one outline level, and Microsoft Word will automatically create a Table of Contents for you, listing all of your chapters by name.

*Note:* If you plan to later make an .ePub format ebook of your print document, *and* if you also plan to use Lulu's free .ePub converter to do so, you will need to use Microsoft Word's default *Heading* styles.

- In the case of chapter titles, you would select your chapter title heading and then apply the "Heading 1" style to it.
- In order to change the "Heading 1" style so that your chapter titles will look as you'd like them to, (with your text still highlighted) right click on the "Heading 1" style in the *Styles and Formatting* panel.
- Make the changes you would like to the style. Then select each of your other chapter titles in the document and apply the "Heading 1" style to them.
- Lulu's .ePub converter will recognize and use a maximum of three heading styles (*Heading 1, 2* and *3*) to convert Microsoft Word documents into .ePub files. Please see Appendix C for more information about Lulu's .ePub converter.

# Position Chapter Title Headings

nly one last step remains for your chapter title headings. You will want to make sure that each chapter heading is positioned at exactly the same spot on the page as each of your other chapter headings. I cannot say this enough, but consistency of style is a fundamental requirement to separate your book from the pack. Consistency of style is key to producing a professional looking product.

Experiment until you find a line position for the chapter title heading that you like (check in *Print Preview* often to see how it looks), and then select and copy the paragraph marks immediately preceding it. Go to the next chapter in your book, select all of the paragraph marks immediately preceding the chapter title heading text, delete them, and then replace them with the paragraph formatting that you copied from Chapter One. (Be certain not to delete any section breaks!)

In addition, make sure that the number (and point size) of the paragraph returns following the chapter heading are exactly the same, as well. Please see the images on the next page for examples.

The number of paragraph returns preceding the Prologue and Chapter One headings are the same in each picture—eight paragraph returns. Likewise, the paragraph returns following the chapter headings match as well—three paragraph returns. The point size and font for each paragraph return are identical on each page.

## Chapter Heading Example One

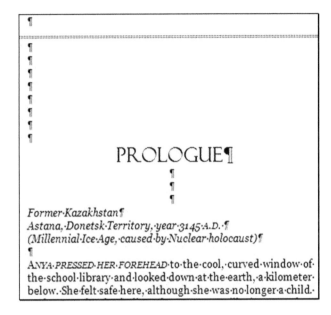

## Chapter Heading Example Two

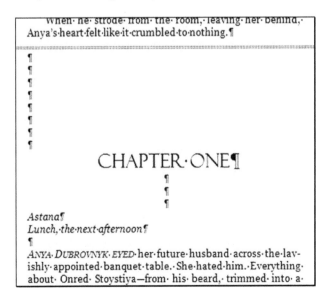

*Note:* It is possible to achieve this same effect by modifying the ChapterHeading style, choosing *Format*, and adjusting the point spacing before and after the ChapterHeading text. You would still need to go through the document to remove any extra paragraph returns, however. The only reason I do not recommend this method is because Smashwords has stringent rules about maximum point sizes allowed in a manuscript. If the point size is too large, your manuscript will be rejected. (However, you could use this method, as long as you remember to readjust the point spacing of your chapter heading style while formatting your ebook document.)

Be sure to save your manuscript!

# Headers or Footers

*N*ow for the fun part! Headers. Although footers will not be addressed in this section, you can apply the information in this chapter to footers, as well.

You will probably want different headers for the odd pages and the even pages of your book. Many styles are possible, but I will explain how to achieve two. In both examples, the page numbers are positioned flush with the left margin for the even pages, and flush with the right margin for the odd pages.

The techniques described in this chapter can be applied to the header text for each of the following two images. The technique used is the same for both.

## Text Justified to the Left or Right

## Centered Headers

Here's how to access the Header:

1. In Microsoft Word 2003, go to *View,* and then select *Header and Footer.*
2. In Microsoft Word 2010 go to the *Insert* tab and click *Header.* Select "Blank." (If you currently have headers in your document which you would like to modify, click "Edit Header" at the bottom of the panel, instead.) I find it easiest to work with one page onscreen at a time, and adjust the page zoom accordingly to make that happen.

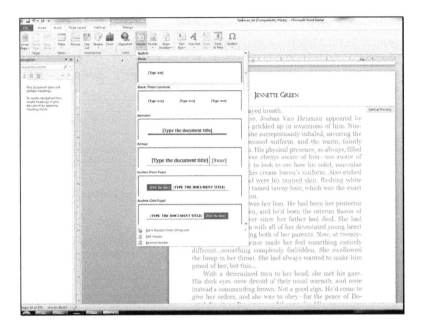

In Microsoft Word 2003, the *Header and Footer* toolbar will show up. In both versions of Microsoft Word, your cursor will automatically go to the first header in your manuscript. Most likely this is your title page. You do not want to insert a header there, so scroll down until you find the first page on which you would like to display a header. This will probably be the page following Chapter One, which means it will be an even number. (Do *not* insert a header on the first page of the chapter!)

## Left/Even Header

Place your cursor in the *Even Page Header* box.

## Microsoft Word 2003 Header
*Header section is enlarged below*

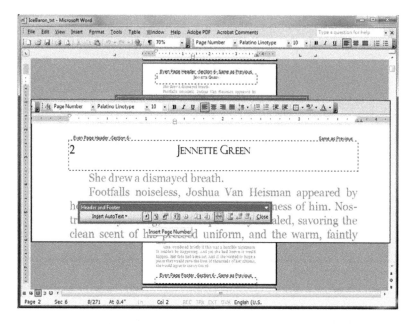

You will notice several things in this picture. First of all, when the cursor is in the box, the left justified paragraph button is highlighted in the top toolbar.

> *Tip:* You can make certain that the header is left-justified in Microsoft Word 2010 by going to *Page Layout*, and clicking the down arrow next to *Paragraph*. Under *Indents and Spacing* and next to "Alignment," select "Left."

## Microsoft Word 2010 Header
*Header section is enlarged below*

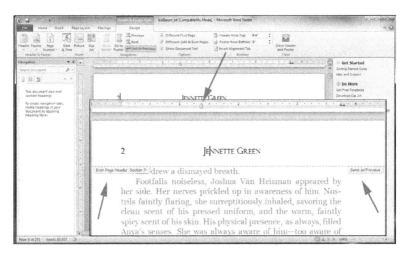

The editable Header section on the page is labeled "Even Page Header" on the left side, and "Same as Previous" on the other. The first is self-explanatory, and the second can be adjusted if you want different, custom headers for each chapter. This may occur if you have a Table of Contents that you'd like to number separately from the rest of the document, and perhaps number with Roman numerals. I'll explain how to do this a little later.

Another thing to notice is the hanging left indent in the ruler toolbar. It is the tiny square box with a triangle pointing upward on top of it. (The top arrow is pointing to it.) The indent triangle corresponds to the exact indentation of the author name, "Jennette." I adjust the amount of indentation for the centered (or left justified) header by sliding the indent triangle until the header text looks centered, or is positioned where I want it to be. I'll give exact instructions on how to do this in just a moment. First, you'll need to insert the page number.

### Insert a Page Number into the Left/Even Header

Click your mouse in the header box, to the far left, where you would like your page number to be. On the *Header and Footer* toolbar, the

"Insert Page Number" button (the first "#" button) is highlighted in the previous "Microsoft Word 2003 Header" image. Click that button to insert the page number. It should be an even page number!

> *Tip:* In Microsoft Word 2010, make sure the green *Headers & Footers Tools* is selected and active. Put your cursor where you want to insert the page number. Then click on *Page Number*, "Current Position," "Plain Number."

Next, to change the default page number, in Microsoft Word 2003, click on the "Format Page Number" button, which is the third "#" button highlighted in the next image. (In Microsoft Word 2010, click the down arrow next to *Page Number*, and click "Format Page Numbers.") The following box will appear in both versions of Microsoft Word.

### Header Section is Enlarged Below

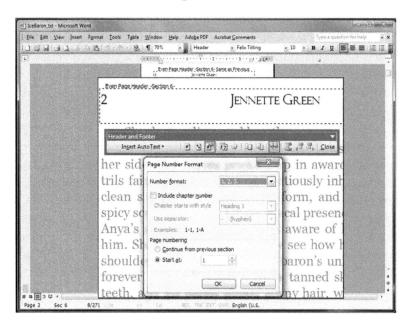

## Here is a Closer Shot of the Previous Image

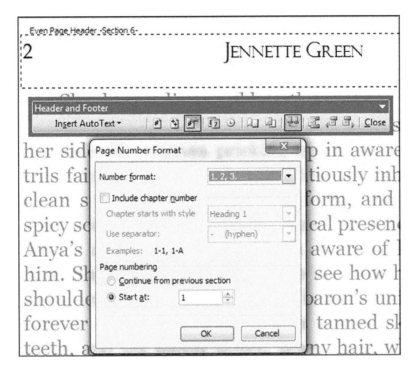

Here, you can choose to continue the page numbering from a previous section. You will probably not select this option, especially if you would like Chapter One to start on page one. Instead, select "Start at:" and put in the page number you'd like the chapter to start with. In this case, I chose to have Chapter One start on page one, which automatically means this first *even* page Header will be page number two.

### Table of Contents Page Numbering

If you insert a Table of Contents into your book, and if you would like to use Roman numerals in that section, you can use the afore-mentioned "Page Number Format" dialogue box to choose the "Number format" for your Table of Contents (TOC). If you do insert TOC page numbering into your document, you will probably not want the TOC page number formatting to carry over into Chapter One.

To prevent this from happening, make sure your mouse is clicked into the Header box for Chapter One. Deselect the "Continue from previous section" button in the "Page Number Format" dialogue box. Alternatively, you could click the "Link to Previous" button (highlighted in the next image for Microsoft Word 2003; the button is on the *Header & Footer* ribbon in Microsoft Word 2010). Then the "Same as Previous" text will disappear from the header section, and the link between the two sections will be broken.

### Before

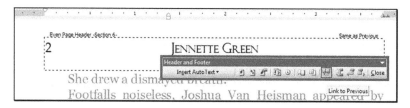

### After

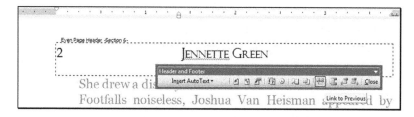

### Insert Header Text into Left/Even Header

Now that the page number has been inserted, let's insert the Header text. Move the hanging left indent triangle/square to a position where you'd like your header text placed. With your cursor in the editable Header text area, just *after* the page number, hit the "Tab" key. The cursor (not the page number) should jump to the "left indent" position. Type your Header text. Move the "left indent" triangle to align it so it looks centered (or is positioned where you want it to look). Check it in *Print Preview*, and adjust as necessary.

The left/even header is finished!

*Tip:* The "Hanging Left Indent" can also be adjusted manually by going to *Format, Paragraph* in 2003 (*Home, Paragraph* in 2010). Click the tab "Indents and Spacing," and under the "Indentation" area, change the "Special" box to "Hanging." Experiment with numbers in the "By" box to see which indentation setting looks best.

## Right/Odd Header

### Insert Header Text into Right/Odd Header

Place your cursor in the *Odd Page Header* box. Remember, do not insert a header on the first page of the chapter.

## *Header Section is Enlarged Below*

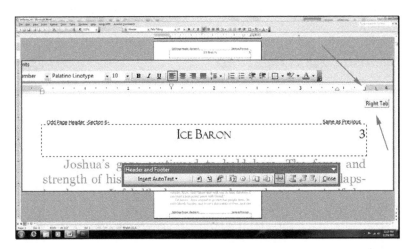

You will note that the text is still left justified. In addition, the "First Line Indent" (the small triangle pointing downward on the toolbar (please note that this is *not* the "hanging left indent" used in the left header section)) is directly above the "Ice" of the title. Move this button to the position where you would like to insert your Header text. The positioning can be adjusted later so it looks either centered, or right-aligned, as depicted in the first image of this chapter. Type your header text.

*Tip:*  The "First Line Indent" can also be adjusted manually by going to *Format, Paragraph* in 2003 (*Home, Paragraph* in 2010). Click the tab "Indents and Spacing," and under the "Indentation" area, change the "Special" box to "First line." Experiment with numbers in the "By" box to see which indentation setting looks best.

### Insert a Page Number into the Right/Odd Header

In the previous image, you can also see a backwards "L" in the ruler bar, which is aligned with the far right margin. (The top arrow is pointing to it.) Below, it says "Right Tab," for the cursor is hovering over the backwards "L." This is the position where you want to insert your page number.

Here is how to insert a "Right Tab" marker into the ruler toolbar, if one is not already located in the proper position. First, make sure your cursor is placed in the right/odd page header box. Then, look at the next image and note the tiny, backwards "L" in the far left margin.

## *Microsoft 2003 Right Tab*

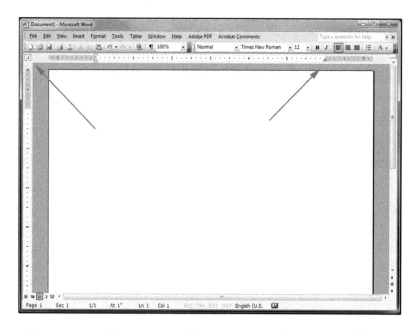

## *2003 Tab Change Button is Enlarged*

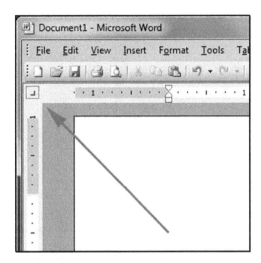

## *Here is the tab change button in 2010*
### *Arrow in left margin is pointing to it*

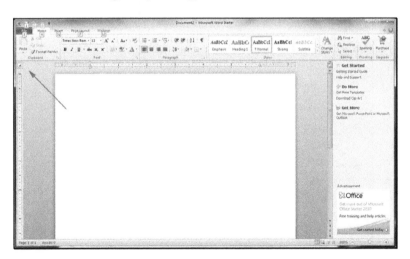

This is the marker for a right tab stop. If it currently does not show a backwards "L" in your ruler's left margin, click on the button until it does. Next, click somewhere in the white area of the ruler toolbar. The new right tab backwards "L" will appear. Drag it until it is located on the far right margin. An enlarged picture of the "Microsoft Word 2003 Right Tab" follows (the arrow is pointing to it).

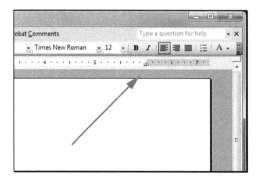

*Note:* The right tab can also be set manually. In 2003, go to *Format, Tabs* (in 2010, go to *Page Layout*, and pull up the *Paragraph* dialogue box; click the "Tabs" button in the bottom left corner). Manually set the position of your right tab. See the following image for an example.

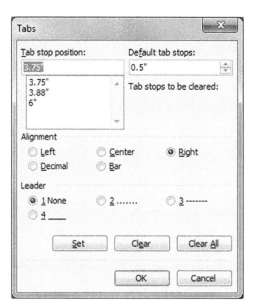

Now, with your cursor at the *end* of your Header text, press the "Tab" key. Your cursor should jump to the far right margin. Insert a page number there.

Your page numbers should now be inserted for your entire document. Check in *Print Preview* to make sure the pages are numbered sequentially from the beginning to the end of your book.

*Troubleshooting Tip:* Sometimes the page numbers will restart with page one at the start of each chapter. If this happens, place your cursor in the header at the beginning of that chapter, choose "Page Number Format," and select the button, "Continue from previous section." You may need to do this for both of the chapter's beginning odd and even headers. Repeat for every chapter that exhibits that problem.

# How to Insert a Table of Contents

*Y*ou may wish to insert a Table of Contents (TOC) into your book. The Microsoft Word program makes this very simple. First, place your cursor in the spot where you would like to insert a Table of Contents. Generally, a Table of Contents is located after the title page, copyright page, etc., and before the Preface, Prologue, or Chapter One.

1. In Microsoft Word 2003 go to *Insert, Reference,* "Index and Tables." Choose the tab "Table of Contents."
2. In Microsoft Word 2010 go to the *Reference* tab. In the *Table of Contents* section, click on "Table of Contents," and then click "Insert Table of Contents."

A number of Table of Contents options are available. Experiment until you find a layout you like. To choose the headings that will display in the Table of Contents, go to "Options" in the "Table of Contents" dialogue box, and find the headings you would like.

For example, as mentioned earlier, you might want to place a number "1" in the "TOC level" box next to ChapterHeading, which is the example style name we've used in this book. This would assign the first heading level of the Table of Contents to the ChapterHeading style. Put a number "2" in the style you would like to list as the second level in the Table of Contents, and so on.

Scroll down the whole "TOC level" list and make sure that only the headings you want have numbers in the "TOC levels" boxes next to them. By default, the Microsoft Word program puts a "1" next to "Heading 1," a "2" next to "Heading 2," and so on. Delete the numbers next to these headings if you will not be using them.

To update a Table Contents, simply place your cursor within the TOC text, and press F9.

> *Note:* If you plan to later make an .ePub format ebook of your print document, *and* if you also plan to use Lulu's free .ePub converter to do so, you will need to use Microsoft Word's default *Heading* styles. Of course, you may modify these styles so your headings will look the way you'd like them to. Please see Appendix C for more information about Lulu's .ePub converter.

# Adding Specialized Formatting to Your Print Document

So far, you've built your print document with a view to converting it later into ebook formats. This print/ebook document is ready now. However, perhaps you would like to add extra formatting to your print document which the ebook formats may not support, such as superscript, drop caps, etc. Now is the time to make those changes to your print document.

First, save your print document as a different name, in order to make an ebook copy that you can edit later (perhaps it could be named MyBookKindle). As mentioned, it's best to save this ebook copy now, before you add the extra formatting to your print file. I like to save my ebook files in a separate folder, just to keep them separate from the print document. Use this newly saved .doc file as your ebook copy. You will take the final steps in the next part of this book to make it fully compliant to ebook standards.

Now you are free to reopen your *print* document and add specialized formatting to your book.

# CreateSpace Templates

reateSpace provides ready-made templates that you can use to create your book. Templates are available for all trim sizes, and two options are available for each.

The first option is a blank template, which includes one blank page into which you can paste your document.

The second option is a "blank template with sample formatted content." This template includes a title page, dedication, acknowledgements, table of contents, and first chapter. It also includes section breaks between the different pages. Simply copy and paste your text into the appropriate sections. However, first turn on the Show/Hide formatting marks. Be certain that you do not delete any section breaks as you insert your text.

You may wish to change the page setup options, as detailed previously in this book, or you may choose to leave them alone. Either is your choice.

Find the CreateSpace interior templates here:

*https://www.createspace.com/Products/Book/InteriorPDF.jsp*

# Final Check of Your Document

Carefully check through your entire document for formatting consistency, and for other possible errors. Although this is by no means an exhaustive list, here are few things to check as you carefully go through your document in *Print Preview*:

1. Are headers printed on the correct pages? (And not printed on the title page, other front matter pages, or the first page of each chapter.)
2. Are pages in the document sequentially numbered from beginning to end? Are the headers positioned correctly on each page?
3. Looking at the two pages side by side in Print Preview, does the first line of text on each page line up with the top line of body text on the next, facing page? (The text at the bottom of the page may not line up—that is okay, and to be expected if you have eliminated widows and orphans.)
4. Check to make sure that no words are "squeezed" together to look like one word. (As mentioned in the "Refine Justification" section.)
5. Check the hyphenation in your document. Are any hyphenated words split between two pages—one half on one page, and half on the next? If so, eliminate the hyphen.
6. Is all of the body text the same font and size?
7. Are all of the chapter title headings the same font and size? Are they placed at exactly the same location on the first page of each chapter?

8. If you have other headings, specially formatted paragraphs or numbered lists, are they formatted exactly as they should be?

9. Does a chapter end with one or two lines on a page? If so, you may need to go back and adjust the character spacing for a previous paragraph.

- Look at the previous pages of your book in *Print Preview*. Choose a paragraph with a very short word at the end, which, if it were instead positioned at the end of the previous line, could pull the whole document up a line, and solve your problem at the end of the chapter.

- Close *Print Preview*. Next, select that entire paragraph. Character spacing can be accessed through *Format, Font* in Microsoft Word 2003 (*Home, Font,* "Advanced" tab in Microsoft Word 2010) and under the "Character Spacing" tab.

- Choose "Spacing: Condensed" and "By: 0.1 pt." See if that helps. If not, undo, and try a different paragraph. Sometimes nothing will help, and you will either have to accept the lonely line(s) at the end of the chapter, or edit the text. Remember, if you adjust the character spacing, you will need to note this change, and undo it in your ebook copy.

Does everything look terrific? If so, congratulations!

You are ready to print your file to PDF for Lightning Source and CreateSpace. You are one giant step closer to becoming published!

# To Do List for Formatting a Print Book

1. Set book trim size, margins, and page layout options
2. Set up body text. Set first line indent, make sure widow orphan is turned on, justify text, refine justification
3. Hyphenate text
4. Replace manual line breaks, tabs, and extra spaces
5. Insert section breaks to separate front matter pages, and to separate chapters
6. Delete extra paragraph returns before section breaks
7. Format chapter title headings, as well as other headings that might exist in your manuscript. Eliminate first line indents for these headings, set font style and size, maintain consistency in chapter title placement on page, and the placement of the first line of text in each chapter.
8. Format headers and page numbers
9. Do a final check of your document
10. Create a PDF/X-1a:2001 of your document

# Print to PDF

$\mathcal{N}$ ow it is time to print your file into PDF/X-1a:2001 file format. Both Lightning Source and CreateSpace require that files be submitted in this format. The reason is simple: all of the fonts are embedded, which means that the PDF you see on your screen will be the exact same file that the printer sees. This way your book will print exactly as it should. The fonts will remain the same, and all the formatting you have worked so hard to accomplish will print correctly.

Here's how to print to PDF. (You will need Adobe Acrobat 7.0 or higher—preferably Professional—installed on your computer.)

Go to *File,* and choose *Print.* Next, click the arrow down button next to *Printer Name: (Printer* in 2010) and select "Adobe PDF."

## *Microsoft Word 2003*

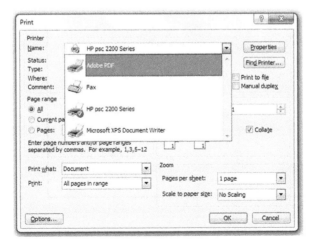

## Microsoft Word 2010

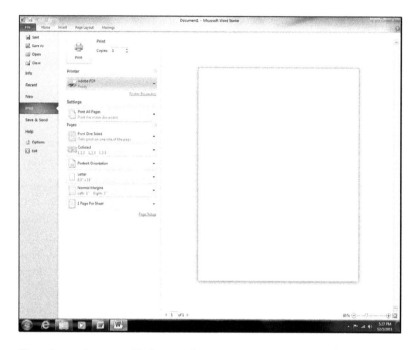

## Previous Image Enlarged

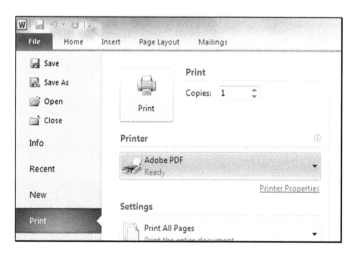

Next, click on *Properties* (*Printer Properties* in Microsoft Word 2010). Click the arrow button next to "Default Settings" and select "PDF/X-1a:2001."

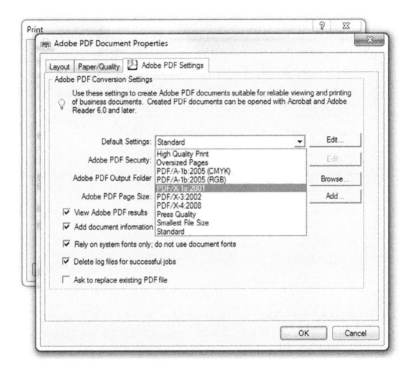

Next, click the "Add" button. In the "Add Custom Paper Size" dialogue box, add a descriptive title under "Page Names," and add your book's trim size to the settings. If your book was 6"x 9" you would type in the following settings (just adjust the numbers to match your book's actual trim size):

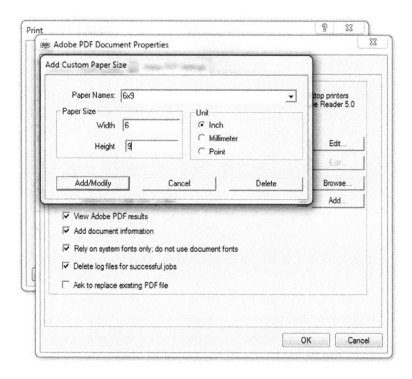

Then click "Add/Modify." If your new "Adobe PDF Page Size" is not showing, click the arrow down button and click on your book trim size. (See the next image for an example.) Click *OK*, and then *OK* again (or *Print*, in Microsoft Word 2010) to print to PDF.

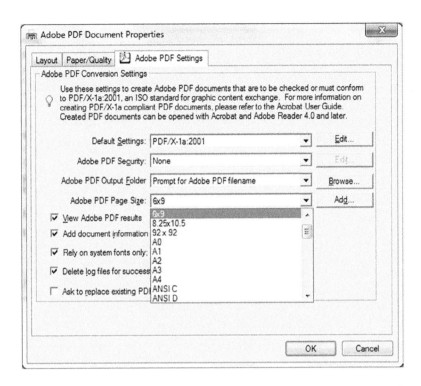

You will be asked to choose a folder to save the file, and you will also be asked to name the file. Lightning Source requires that the file be named *ISBN_txt* (where the ISBN is the unique ISBN for your print book). Do not include dashes in the ISBN. An example might be *9780984404445_txt*. The file can be named *ISBN_txt* for CreateSpace, as well.

Note: If for some reason the print to Adobe PDF function is not working correctly in your Microsoft Word program, go to Appendix A in this book for an alternate method of creating the PDF/X-1a:2001 file for your document.

Your file is finished! You can now check the settings in Adobe Acrobat, to make sure all of the fonts are embedded, and that the file was processed by Acrobat® Distiller®.

To do this, open the file in Adobe Acrobat, and then go to *File*, and click *Properties*.

On the first screen you can check that the "Page Size" is correct. It also details that the file was produced by Acrobat Distiller.

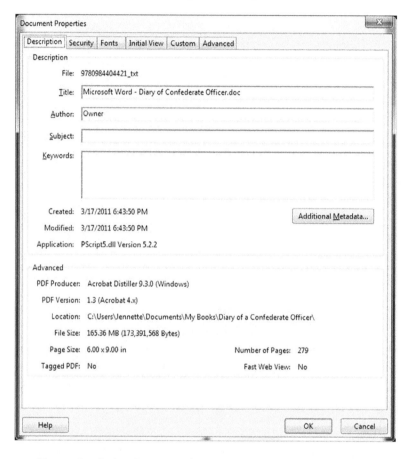

If you check the *Security* tab, "No Security" should be selected, and all options beneath "Document Restrictions Summary" should be "Allowed."

Check the *Fonts* tab. All fonts should be embedded.

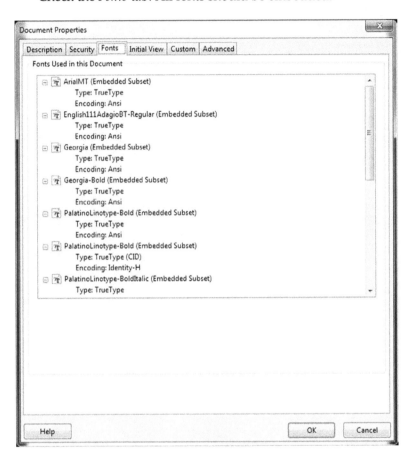

Finally, check the *Custom* tab. The values listed should be PDF/X-1a:2001, as listed in the next image.

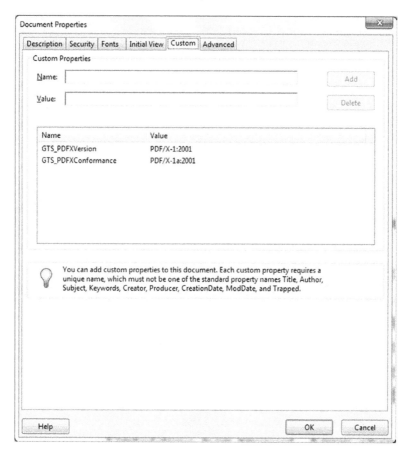

If there are no images in your book, you are finished! Your book block interior is ready to be uploaded to LSI or CS. However, if images are involved, please read on.

## Color vs. Grayscale Images in Book Interior

The cost to print a book with color images on the inside is much higher than to print an interior book block with grayscale images. In fact, both LSI and CreateSpace require that the trim size for a color interior book block be larger than the actual final trim size for your book. This accounts for the bleed of the color images and for trimming the pages to the final trim size.

For example, with LSI, if you want to print a 5.5"x 8.5" book that is illustrated with color images, the page size for the interior book block pages would be 5.75" x 9." This is true even if your color images are small, and do not extend to the edge of the page.

For more information, please visit the following link, pgs. 10, 13:

*http://www1.lightningsource.com/ops/files/pod/LSI_FileCreationGuide.pdf*

Also, see Appendix E, "Lightning Source" section, for more information about color printing options at LSI.

CreateSpace states the following regarding color images on interior book pages:

*"If you want your images to bleed to the edges of your book, ensure that they extend at least .125" beyond the final trim size from the top, bottom and outer edges and submit your PDF .25" higher and .125" wider than your selected trim size to accommodate the full bleed area."*

Please see the following link for more information:

*https://www.createspace.com/Products/Book/InteriorPDF.jsp*

### Convert Images to Grayscale with Adobe Acrobat Pro

Since color interior books cost more than black and white books to print, you may want to convert your color images to grayscale for your book interior. You can do so in Adobe Acrobat Pro. Go to *Advanced, Print Production,* and click on *Preflight.* (In Acrobat X, go to *Tools, Print Production,* and then click on *Preflight.*)

Click on the arrow next to "PDF Fixups," click on "Convert to grayscale," and then, in the bottom right corner of the box, click on "Analyze and fix." It will prompt you to save your document as a new file name. Be aware that the output may be grainy, depending upon the quality of your images. See the next section for a better method to convert images to black and white.

*Note:* The method mentioned above works for Acrobat Pro 9 and later versions. Prior versions of the software may convert the text to a dark gray color, which is less than 100% black. Here's how to check: After you've converted your PDF/X-1a:2001 file to grayscale, check the black color of your fonts by going to *Advanced, Print Production,* and choose *Output Preview.* Hover your cursor over the black text in your document (you may need to zoom in on the text in order to get a good reading) and check the levels in the CMYK panel. The level for "Process Black" should be 100%. If it is not, you may need to use another method to convert your images to grayscale.

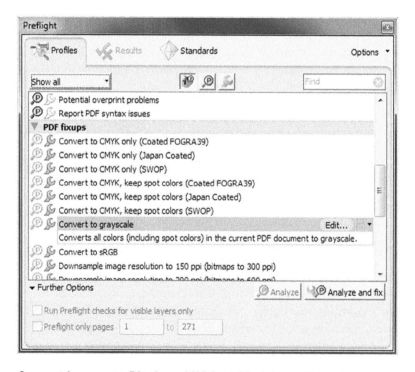

## Convert Images to Black and White with Adobe Photoshop

If your images are of high quality, you may want to manually control the conversion of each picture to grayscale. This will produce a higher quality output, resulting in grayscale tones that will more closely match the color variations of your original color images. To do this, you will need to convert each of your images to black and white in a program such as Adobe Photoshop, and then reinsert them into your document. (Then you will need to remake the PDF/X-1a:2001 file, as previously described.)

If you're working with RGB images, in Photoshop go to *Image, Adjustments,* and select "Black and White." Then adjust the six sliders in the "Black and White" dialogue box until you're pleased with the resulting image. You can also go to the *Adjustments* panel to add an adjustment layer. Click the "Black and White" icon.

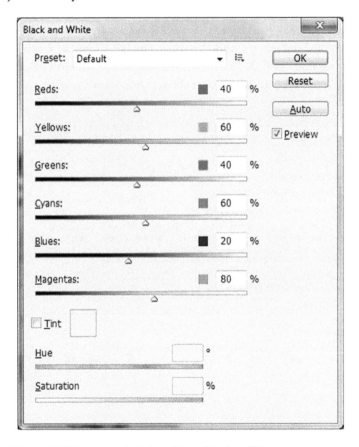

## Save Your PDF as an Adobe PostScript File

Next, if images are involved in a file, I like to save the original PDF file as an Adobe® PostScript® file (.ps), and then process it with Acrobat Distiller. I am not sure if this step is really necessary, but if you would like to make certain that your file will be accepted by LSI or CS, it's simple to do.

Go to *File,* and choose *Save As.* Leave the file name the same, and hit the arrow down button next to "save as type." Choose the PostScript ".ps" extension and save.

Close the PDF file that you have open (or you will get an error message with the next step), but leave the Adobe Acrobat program open.

Next, go back to *Advanced, Print Production* (n Acrobat X, go to *Tools, Print Production*), and this time choose "Acrobat Distiller." Make sure that "PDF/X-1a:2001" is selected in the "Default Settings" for the Acrobat Distiller dialogue box. If not, click the arrow down button and select it.

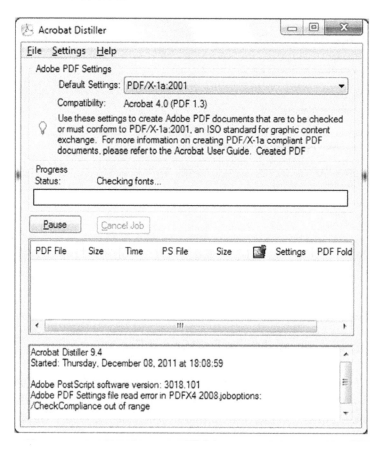

Next, click on *File*, click *Open*, and find the ".ps" file you just saved. Click on it, and then click *Open*. Acrobat Distiller will now process the file so it will meet all PDF/X-1a:2001 specifications. This new file will replace the previous PDF file that you first made from your Microsoft Word .doc.

You can now open the file in Adobe Acrobat again, and check the settings under *File* and then *Properties*, like you did earlier.

## Check Image DPI

One last thing that you will want to do, if you have images in your file, is to check the dpi of the images with Adobe Acrobat Pro. As mentioned earlier in this book, Lightning Source requires that images be 300 dpi, and that line drawings be 600 dpi. The reason for these requirements is simple: anything less may result in poor print quality, and if the dpi is low enough, the output will appear grainy.

It's easy to check the dpi in Adobe Acrobat Pro. Once again, go to *Advanced, Print Production* (in Acrobat X, go to *Tools, Print Production*), and click on "Preflight." You may need to set up a custom profile in order to check the dpi of your images. The next section explains how to do this.

## Set Up a Custom Profile in Preflight

It is very easy to set up a custom profile in "Preflight" so that you will be able to check the specific dpi for each of your images. Here's how:

Click the *Options* button in the top right corner of the Preflight box, and then select *Edit Preflight Profiles*.

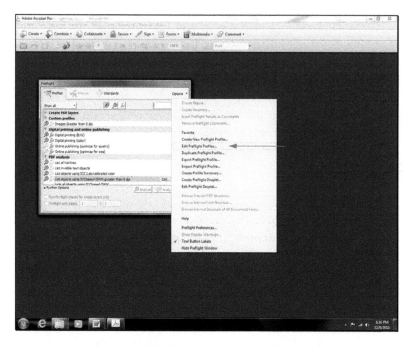

*Previous Image Enlarged*

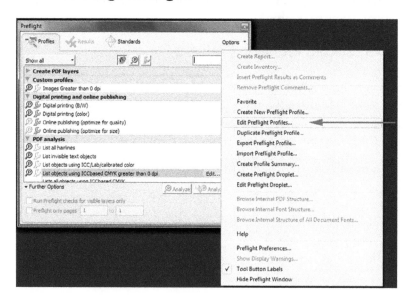

The following box will appear. In the lower left corner, click on the button with a " + " on it in order to create a new Preflight profile.

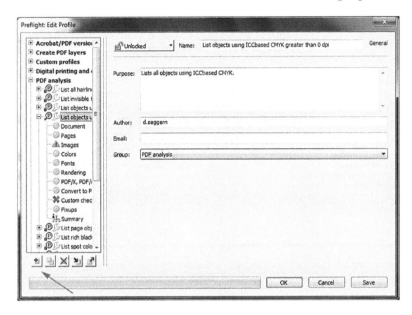

Directly above the " + " button you clicked, you'll see a variety of folders. Click on the " + " next to "Custom profiles." Within "Custom profiles," you'll see a number of items listed. Click on "Images," and the screen image printed at the top of the next page will appear.

Name your file. (I named mine "Images Greater than 0 dpi," since I want this option to list the dpi of every image in the document. This way I can learn several important pieces of information about each image.) Change the settings to zero, to match those in the previous image. To achieve the "!" warning sign, just click the down arrow and select it. Click *OK*, and your new custom profile will be listed under "Custom profiles" in *Preflight*. (See the second image on the next page.)

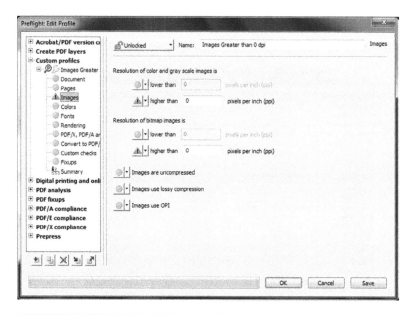

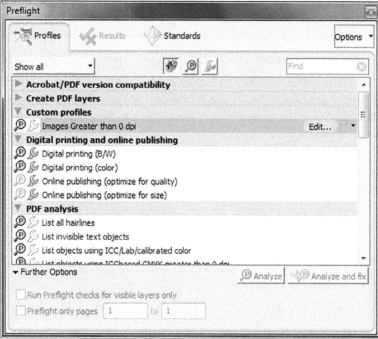

Now you can check the dpi of every image in your document. You can also check to see if the images are CMYK, and either color or "Black" (grayscale). Click on your new, custom profile, so that it is selected. Then click "Analyze" in the lower right portion of the dialogue box (not "Analyze and fix").

In the next screen, click on the little " + " sign next to the yellow " ! " and information about the file will come up. In this particular file, the image point sizes (height and width) are listed, as are the dpi/ppi of the images (199.883 ppi, which is less than the 300 dpi/ppi it should be). It also indicates that the images have been converted to grayscale (hence the "Black" listed). This is a wealth of information, and I use it often to troubleshoot problems with files.

In the case of the following file, I learned that the images in the document needed to be adjusted to 300 dpi before uploading the file to LSI or CS. It is far better to learn this information now and fix it, than to have the file rejected, fix it later, and pay for re-upload costs through LSI!

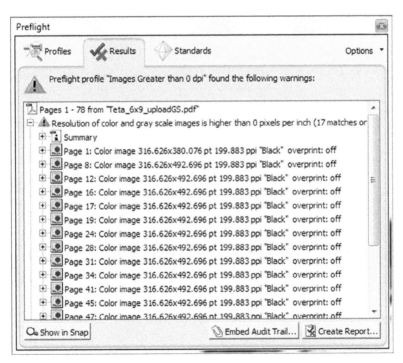

*2*

# Format eBooks

## Overview

As mentioned earlier, I always format my print book files with a view to converting them later into ebook formats. As I will usually convert every print book into an ebook, this makes sense for me.

The three major ebook formats that I will cover in this section include: Kindle, Barnes & Noble, and Smashwords. A chapter about files for LSI's ebook program is included, as well.

I always create the Kindle file first, and then use that base file to create the other file formats. When I explain how to format the Kindle file, you will notice that I'll also take into account Barnes & Noble and Smashwords' requirements. Smashwords has a style guide that is helpful for converting any document into an ebook format. I've found that if I follow their guidelines, all of my ebooks turn out right the first time.

Before we get started, it may be helpful to know that Kindle, Barnes & Noble's NOOK, and Smashwords all have different maximum file sizes. If you have a number of images in your book, this will be of particular interest to you. Image compression can be applied to your pictures to reduce the file size, if needed. More on this topic is located under the section entitled, "More About Images in Your eBook," on page 113.

For now, please note that the maximum file sizes are:

1.   Kindle – 50 megabytes
2.   Barnes & Noble's NOOK – 20 megabytes
3.   Smashwords – 5 megabytes

Formatting ebook files is surprisingly simple, as long as you follow *all* of the steps. Let's start with Kindle.

# Kindle Format

*T*he first thing you will want to do is open your print book .doc or .docx file that you have just completed. Using the "save as" function, rename it, in order to preserve your perfect print file. Perhaps naming your ebook file "MyBookKindle" would be helpful. I also like to save my ebook files in a separate folder. It helps to keep them all in one place, and separate from the print file.

As you're saving your file, please keep in mind that Smashwords only accepts the Microsoft Word .doc format. *Not* the .docx format. If you're working in Microsoft Word 2010, now would be a good time to save your document as a .doc file. Use that .doc file as you work through the ebook section of this book.

## Delete Optional Hyphens and Manually Adjusted Character Spacing

Before you begin, take a look at your notes. Did you add any optional hyphens (manual hyphens)? Did you adjust the character spacing for a paragraph or two? Did you add extra spaces to a paragraph? Now is the time to delete all of those changes.

## Replace Specialized Scene Break Symbols with Asterisks

You may have inserted a series of special symbols in your book in order to separate scene breaks. In my romance novel, *The Commander's Desire*, I used a series of swords to separate scenes, as I liked how they looked, and because swords are a theme in the book.

> She heaved a great breath and stared at him, struggling to find a way to win the advantage over this man.
>
> ∤ ∤ ∤ ∤ ∤
>
> The Commander looked at Elwytha with her dark hair and flashing, brilliant blue eyes. A beauty. This fact stabbed into his calloused soul. And she clearly found him abhorrent. That

To my chagrin, however, the symbols showed up on the iPad and Kindle as a series of square boxes. Now, for my ebooks, I replace these special characters with asterisks.

## Mirror Margins and Headers

Ebooks do not have headers or page numbers. Mirror margins are also unnecessary. So the first thing you will want to do is go back to *File, Page Setup* (in 2010 go to the *Page Layout* tab, then *Page Setup*). Choose to apply the settings to the "whole document," and then change the "Mirror Margins" setting to "Normal." I also prefer to even up the margins, so they are roughly the same all the way around. I keep the paper size same as in the print edition.

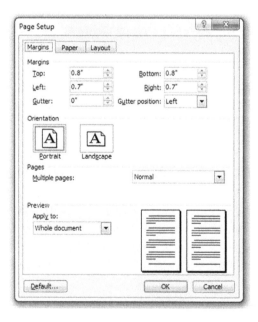

Next, go to *View, Header and Footer* (in 2010 go to the *Insert* tab, then *Header*, and click "Edit Header" at the bottom of the panel). Scroll through your document until you find your first header, which will be an even page header. Delete everything in the header box. Next, go to the odd page header, and delete everything in that box. Check through the rest of the document to make sure that all headers are deleted. Close the *Header and Footer* toolbar.

## Single Space the Document

If you did not already do so when formatting your print book, now is the time to make sure your entire document is single-spaced. This setting can eliminate conflicting formatting that might cause problems later, in the final ebook versions. Select all of the text in your entire document ("Ctrl + A") and make sure that "line spacing" is set to "single" in the *Paragraph* dialogue box.

## Replace Section Breaks with Page Breaks

Ebooks work best if page breaks are used, instead of section breaks. It's easy to change section breaks into page breaks with Microsoft Word's *Replace* command.

Go to *Edit, Replace* (in Microsoft Word 2010, go to the *Home* tab, and in the *Editing* section, click *Replace*). Place "^b" (no quotes) in the "Find what" box, and "^m" in the "Replace with" box. Click "Replace All."

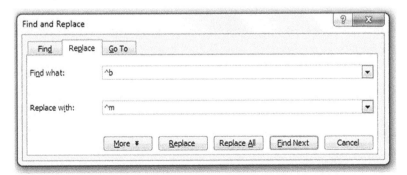

Turn on the formatting marks (Show/Hide). Quickly scroll through your document to ensure that all of the section breaks have been replaced by a page break.

```
----------------------------Page Break----------------------------
```

## Paragraph Returns

Here is where we will begin to incorporate Smashwords' requirements into the file. To find the most recent version of the *Smashwords Style Guide,* follow this link:

*http://www.smashwords.com/books/view/52*

One Smashwords requirement is to "Never use more than four consecutive paragraph returns" (pg. 5). The guide states that extra paragraph returns can create blank pages in ebooks.

> *Tip:* By the way, if you choose to do block formatting for paragraphs (blocks of text separated by white space, instead of using paragraph indents), I highly recommend reading page 5 in the *Smashwords Style Guide*, or else read the section in this book entitled, "How to Include Extra Spacing After Block Paragraphs," on page 108.

Go to *Edit, Replace* (in Microsoft Word 2010, go to the *Home* tab, and in the *Editing* section, click *Replace*). Place "^p^p^p^p^p" in the *Find* box. Click "Find Next." Slowly go through your document, looking for five paragraph returns. Modify each instance, so no more than four consecutive paragraph returns exist in a given location. On the next page are "before" and "after" examples:

*Before*

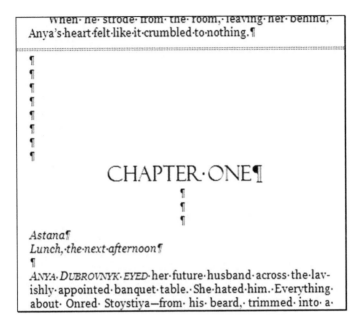

*After*

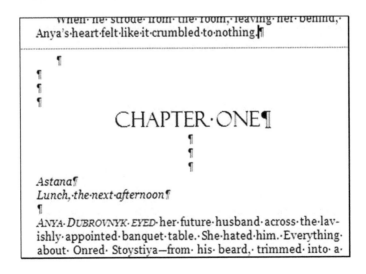

**How to Include Extra Spacing After Block Paragraphs**

This section is entirely optional for books with indented paragraphs. Books with block paragraphs, separated by white space, should always follow Smashwords' formatting rules, as explained in the following paragraphs.

Smashwords recommends that a publisher should not separate block paragraphs with an extra (blank) paragraph return between them. Instead, they recommend separating paragraphs by modifying the line spacing before and after the block paragraphs. In order to do this, you must first make sure that all of the body text of your book is formatted with the same style.

Then, select your body paragraph style in the *Styles and Formatting* panel, right click, and then click "Select All # Instance(s)." Next, right click the style again and choose "Modify," and then click on the "Format" button in the new dialogue box. Click on "Paragraph." Now modify the line spacing before and after each paragraph. Six points before, and six points after might work just fine. Perhaps you would like 12 points better. Check it in *Print Preview* to see which looks best.

As mentioned before, any publisher using indented paragraphs can ignore this section, unless you'd like a small space separating all of the paragraphs in the ebook edition of your book. If you look at the free preview sections of ebooks on Kindle, you will notice that many major publishers separate indented paragraphs by a little bit of white space. It is not a necessary requirement, but if the aesthetics of this formatting technique appeals to you, it is an option to try. (Do *not* go back and change the paragraph formatting in your print book, however. This technique is *not* used in print books.)

Do not mix block and indented paragraphs for Smashwords ebooks, or you will receive an error message when the file is uploaded.

By the way, you do not need a Kindle reader in order to take a look at Kindle books published by major publishers. To view the free sample previews for Kindle on a PC, download Amazon's free "Kindle for PC" software.

*http://www.amazon.com/gp/feature.html/ref=kcp_pc_mkt_lnd?docl d=1000426311*

## Additional Rules and Recommendations

Other warnings listed in Smashwords' faq material (pgs. 9–10 of the style guide) and on Barnes & Noble's ebook recommendations page apply to all ebook formats. These include:

1. No large font sizes (11–12 points is recommended, with a maximum size of 14 pt.)
2. No exotic fonts. Recommended fonts are Times New Roman, Garamond, and Arial. I've also had good luck with Georgia.
3. No text wrapping around floating images
4. Avoid multiple paragraph styles for the body text (don't mix Normal with Body Text, for example). ***Sometimes a file will be rejected by Smashwords because multiple "body" styles are present in the text. In that extreme instance, select all of the text in your document and change it to Times New Roman. Then go through and reformat your front matter and chapter title headings so they are the correct size and font.
5. No footnotes. (Footnotes, endnotes and indexes are possible in ebooks, but the formatting directions for these are not covered in this book. In short, you could add bookmarks and hyperlinks to link to endnotes and/or indexes. Anchors can also be used, but again, if these elements are necessary in your document, I'd recommend purchasing an advanced Kindle formatting book.)
6. No tabs or spaces used to format or indent text (remember, we already replaced these with first line indents when formatting the print book).
7. Separate paragraphs with only one paragraph return. In other words, at the end of one paragraph, hit return one time, and begin the new paragraph. Two consecutive paragraph returns will cause large spaces between paragraphs. If you want extra spacing between paragraphs, please see the previous section, entitled, "How to Include Extra Spacing After Block Paragraphs," on page 108. Don't mix block paragraphs with indented paragraphs for Smashwords.

8. Do not use Microsoft Word's "All Caps" or "Small Caps" function. They do not carry over to ebook formats, and will show up as all lowercase letters. Instead, use the Caps Lock key to type text in all capital letters.

9. Do not use superscripts, subscripts, and most symbols, for they don't translate well to ebook formats. (For example, use "1/2" or "1/4" or "1st," instead of the auto-formatted fraction character.)

10. No text in columns, tables, or text boxes. (Note: New Kindle documentation states that Microsoft Word tables *are* supported. They are not supported in Smashwords files, however.) Tables, text boxes, and other graphic elements can be converted into images and reinserted into the document, if necessary. Here's how:

**Convert a Table, Chart, Graph, or Text Box into an Image**

- If your table (or other graphic element) is in a Microsoft Word document, print the page to PDF. If you are unable to save one page as a PDF, save the entire document as a PDF.
- If your table is in a multiple page PDF, note which page it is on.
- Open an image software program, such as Photoshop or Gimp, that will allow you to open a PDF file. As you open the PDF file, choose the following settings, if available: 1) specify which page you would like to open, 2) the dpi you would like your final image to be, and 3) if available, choose the color space (RGB or CMYK) that you would like your final image to be.
- Using the crop tool, crop the table from the page. If needed, adjust the image resolution and resize the image. Save the table image as a JPG file.
- Insert the image into your Microsoft Word .doc.

Whew! Those are a lot of rules. I highly recommend skimming through the *Smashwords Style Guide* for more useful tips.

Thankfully, we took care of most of these issues earlier in this book, by choosing formatting styles that are within Smashwords' ranges.

## Turn Off AutoCorrect Options

Now is a good time to turn off Microsoft Word's *AutoCorrect* features. This way, if you replace all instances of "1st" in your document with the plain number and letters, the Microsoft Word program will not undo all of your hard work and automatically change it back to the superscript version.

1. In Microsoft Word 2003 go *Tools, AutoCorrect Options*.
2. In Microsoft Word 2010 go to *File,* and under *Help* click *Options*. In the next dialogue box that appears, click on *Proofing*. Under the *AutoCorrect options* section, click the button entitled, "AutoCorrect Options."

In both versions of Microsoft Word, under the "AutoFormat" tab, uncheck the four boxes under "Apply." Under the "AutoFormat as You Type" tab, uncheck the "Ordinals" and "Fractions" boxes.

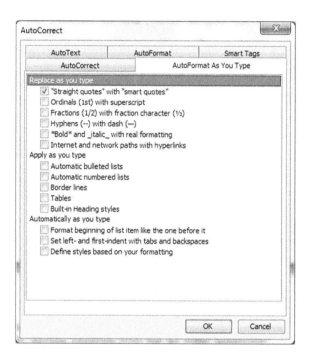

## Change Font Sizes of Chapter Headings and Titles

The title page, chapter headings, and perhaps a few other headings in your book probably have fonts that are larger than Smashwords' recommended 14 pt. maximum. Now is the time to change these font sizes in the *Styles and Formatting* panel.

For example, click on the "ChapterHeading" (or "Header 1") style formatted earlier in this book, right click it, and then choose "Select All # Instance(s)." Right click the style again, and choose "Modify," and then change the point size. All of the chapter title headings in your book should now be the correct font size.

Manually change the font sizes in the front matter of your book, including the title page, dedication, and so on. Last of all, check through your document in *Print Preview* to make sure that all text has been changed.

I have had good luck using 16 pt. fonts for titles with Smash-words, but to be safe, you might want to follow Smashwords' recommended 14 pt. maximum font.

You are almost finished formatting your ebook. Only two items remain for the Kindle version.

> *Tip:* As mentioned earlier, if you've used a title font that prints in All Caps, retype the text with the caps lock key on. Otherwise, the letters will show up as lowercase in the ebook versions.

## Insert a Cover Image into Your eBook

You may wish to insert a JPG image of your book cover into the beginning of your document. If you would like to do this, be sure to place the image into the file in Microsoft Word 2003 or 2010 via the *Insert* menu (*Insert, Picture,* (and choose "From File" in 2003)). After you've inserted the image, add a page break "Ctrl + Enter" after the picture. Kindle documentation states that publishers should not copy and paste a picture into an ebook document.

If, for some reason, your cover does not show up in the document after you have inserted it, go to page 197 for possible solutions to the problem.

## More About Images in Your eBook

Kindle and PubIt! (NOOK) support JPG, GIF and non-transparent PNG files. Kindle KF8 (advanced formatting) documentation recommends using color images, if possible, and to use the JPG format for photos, and the GIF format for line images. KF8 also recommends 300 dpi/ppi images, in an effort to look forward to the future capabilities of the Kindle devices. However, as of now, 300 dpi resolution is not available on any Kindle device.

> "Dpi" stands for "dots per inch," (for print files) and "ppi" stands for "pixels per inch" (for computer screens). Although they are not technically the same thing, they are close enough for our purposes, and I will use "dpi" for simplicity's sake here.

PubIt! recommends that images be "optimized for web delivery." No specific dpi is indicated in their documentation. Images on the web are generally 72 dpi. Therefore, the range of 72 to 300 dpi leaves a lot of wiggle room to choose from for your image files!

Choosing the correct dpi for your images can be a difficult decision. You must weigh the size of your file (higher dpi generally creates clearer images, but large file sizes) vs. the needs of your customers. Make certain your images are good enough to be seen clearly. Check the output in the Kindle Enhanced Previewer and in the NOOK for PC previewer (see the next paragraph). In addition, take into consideration the ebook file size limits imposed by the different online retailers. See Appendix E for complete information on the ebook file sizes allowed at the different online retailers.

By the way, the link to download Kindle's "Enhanced Previewer" can be found on the KDP platform. Set up a new title. Once you have uploaded your Microsoft Word .doc zip file, two options will appear under #6 "Preview Your Book." Look for the option to download the "Enhanced Previewer." A similar option to download the NOOK for PC previewer becomes available after you upload your book to the PubIt! platform. Both are excellent tools to check your ebooks, and I have found them quite valuable.

One last thought. While choosing the size, dpi, and image file type for your ebook pictures, please keep in mind that the maximum image size for the Kindle is 600 x 800 pixels. The maximum image size for the NOOK is 600 x 730 pixels. Typically, the eReader devices will automatically size the image smaller, so that it will fit within the screen area.

If your book has a number of images, and you realize that your document file is larger than Kindle, PubIt!, or Smashwords will accept, consider adjusting your images by converting them to JPGs (if they are currently in a different format), and compressing the image. Always check the final output, however. Sometimes compressing images can result in poor quality.

For detailed information on adjusting images and reducing your ebook's file size, visit Kindle's FAQ, entitled, "Reducing Your Book Content File Size." It is located at the following link:

*https://kdp.amazon.com/self-publishing/*
*help?topicId=AQY9VBML4LKPK*

## Create a Table of Contents for Your eBook

You may also want to include a hyperlinked Table of Contents (TOC) in your ebooks, even if you did not include a TOC in your print edition. Readers of ebooks can click on this hyperlinked TOC and go to any chapter or section of the book that they would like.

### Kindle Table of Contents

Kindle accepts the automatically generated Table of Contents that is created by the Microsoft Word program. This Table of Contents links to the different chapters and sections in your book. For information on how to insert a Table of Contents into your document, please go to the chapter entitled, "How to Insert a Table of Contents," located on page 76, in *Part One* of this book.

However, for the ebook version of your book, be sure to turn off the page numbers listed on the Table of Contents page (uncheck "Show page numbers," as shown in the next image) or else they will show up on Kindle's TOC page. The page numbering in a Microsoft Word .doc does not correspond to page numbering in reflowable text eReaders, such as Kindle or NOOK.

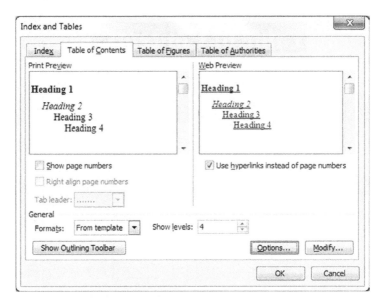

Kindle guidelines require that three "Guide Items" be placed in your Kindle document. These items can be accessed through the Kindle reader's "Go To" menu. The three areas that must be marked by guides in your document are the cover, the Table of Contents, and the beginning of your book. You will need to create a bookmark for each of these areas. Here is how to do it:

1. First, you will go to your Table of Contents page. With your cursor, select the heading, "Table of Contents" (or whatever you named that section of your book). Then go to *Insert, Bookmark,* and then label the bookmark "toc" (without the quotes). Click "Add."
2. Next, go the start of your document and with your cursor, select/highlight the heading for that section. It might be the Prologue, Introduction, Chapter One; whichever section you feel is the start of your book. Add a bookmark and name it "start" (without the quotes). Click "Add."
3. Last of all, click on the cover that you probably placed in the beginning of your book. Name the bookmark "cover" (without the quotes). Click "Add."

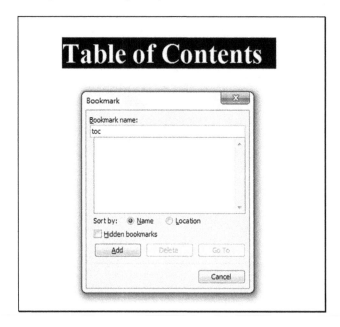

### Smashwords Table of Contents Rules

The *Smashwords Style Guide* emphatically states that the Table of Contents generated automatically by Microsoft Word should not be used for the files submitted to their website. More about the Smashwords Table of Contents can be found in the "Smashwords Format" section, on page 125.

## Delete the Print ISBN from the eBook Copyright Page

You've assigned an ISBN to your print book, and it is listed on the copyright page. It will need to be deleted from your ebook. Each different book format requires a new ISBN. If you have an ISBN for your ebook, insert it in place of the print ISBN.

The good news is that Amazon and Barnes & Noble do not require an ISBN for ebooks. They assign their own internal control number to your file, instead. In this case, simply delete all reference to an ISBN from your copyright page.

## Convert Your Microsoft Word File to Kindle Format

Congratulations! Your book is now formatted for Kindle! You are almost finished.

Now it is time to turn your Microsoft Word document into a Kindle zip file, ready for upload to Amazon's KDP Platform.

*http://kdp.amazon.com/*

Make a new folder on your computer. I choose to name the folder "Kindlefiles" (without quotes, of course), because that makes sense to me. Next, make a new zip file and name it "Kindlefiles," too.

> *Tip:* If you do not know how to make a zip file, go to *Windows Explorer,* click on *File, New,* and then choose "Compressed (zipped) Folder." *Please note:* Your Kindlefiles zip file **must** be spelled *exactly* the same way as the Kindlefiles folder!

Now you'll save your Microsoft Word .doc as a Kindle file. Go to *File, Save As,* and then choose "Web Page, filtered." (*Not* "Single file web page" or "Web page") If the program gives you a warning, click "Yes" to continue the save.

As you're saving the file, Microsoft Word will allow you the option of giving the book a title. This title corresponds to the <title> tag in an html document. Name it your book title. You also have the option to change the file name of your work. Name it "Kindlefiles," too, if you like, or any name with no spaces in the title.

> **Important!** Be sure to save the file in the Kindlefiles *folder* you just created!

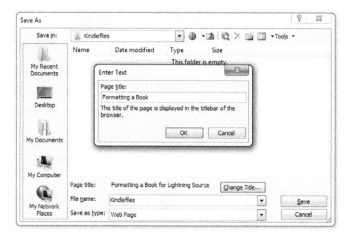

When you have saved the file, a page that looks like a web page (html page) will come up on the screen.

If you have a Table of Contents with hyperlinks, you may wish to test them now to make sure they work correctly. Next, exit out of that html file and go to the folder which contains your Kindlefiles folder and the Kindlefiles zip file.

Double-click on the Kindlefiles folder. Go to *File, Edit,* and "Select All." Then again go to *File, Edit,* and now select "Copy."

Go back up a folder until you see your Kindlefiles zip file. Double-click the zip file folder and paste your files inside. Now your zip file is completed!

Note: If your ebook will contain no images, it is not necessary to make a zip file. Simply save your .doc as a filtered web page, and then upload that .htm file to the KDP Platform.

## Upload to Amazon's KDP Platform

Now go to Amazon's KDP Platform:

*(http://kdp.amazon.com/)*

Navigate to your "Bookshelf." Click the "Add new title" button near the top of the page in order to set up a new title.

The first screen that comes up allows you to input information about your title. You will have plenty of time to browse this page and make your selections. However, at this point, we are only interested in Step Five. Browse for your Kindlefiles *zip* file and click the "Upload book" button. (You may or may not want to enable digital rights management. I usually do not, but that is up to you.)

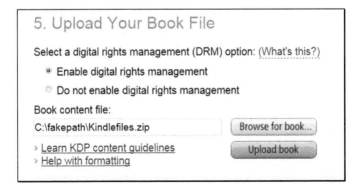

If you have followed all of the steps, your file should upload with no problem.

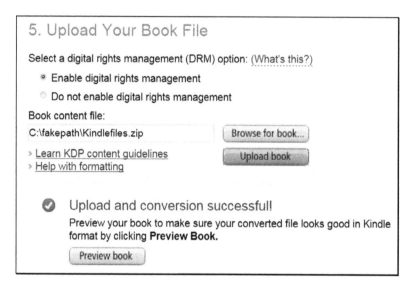

Next a "Preview Your Book" Section will appear. You have the option to preview your book in the "Simple Previewer," which is for books without advanced formatting, or the "Enhanced Previewer," which allows you to see advanced formatting. The "Enhanced Previewer" will also let you see how your book will look on three Kindle devices, as well as the iPhone and iPad. This book does not cover any advanced Kindle formatting, so the "Simple Previewer" may be all you need to view your book.

Note: Even if your book does not contain advanced formatting, you may still want to consider downloading the "Enhanced Previewer." It provides a larger, clearer screen, so you can get a better view of your document. On the KDP page, just click the download button, and then click "Run." After you've installed it, start up the program, and then, back on the KDP page, click the link entitled, "Download Book Preview File." Open that file in the "Enhanced Previewer" and take a look at your book.

- One final note—Sometimes the file downloaded from KDP does not contain the .mobi extension, and the Previewer won't open it. If this is the case, add .mobi to the extension of the file name. In order to do this, first make sure that you can see the file extensions on your computer. To turn on this feature, in Windows Explorer for Microsoft Windows 7 go to *Organize* (or *My Computer* in earlier versions), click on "Folder and Search Options" (or *Tools*, then "Folder Options"), and then click the "View" tab. Uncheck the box next to "Hide extensions for known file types." Now that you can see the file extensions, you can rename your file. An example might be *Kindle-files.mobi*. The Enhanced Previewer will now be able to open the file.

To give the "Simple Previewer" a try, click the "Preview book" button. A Kindle preview screen will appear. The following two images show the upper and lower sections of the Kindle previewer.

In the first image, the left and right arrows allow you to move forward or backward one page at a time in your manuscript. Check your ebook to see how your formatting looks.

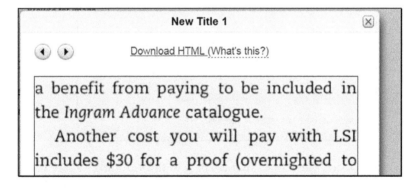

The lower section shows a "Location" area. This is another way to navigate through your book. Just type in numbers and the previewer will take you to that section of the ebook. You can also change the font size (for viewing only), or click on the "Menu" button.

Clicking on the "Menu" button will bring up the following options:

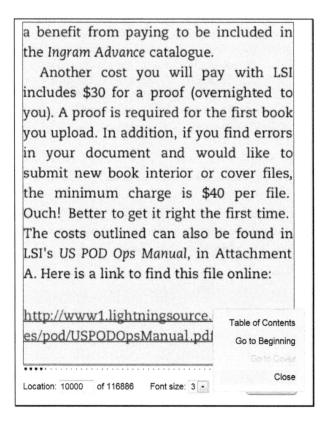

Click on "Table of Contents" or "Go to Beginning" to see if the hyperlinks in your documents work properly. If you click on "Table of Contents," it should take you to your TOC page. "Go to Beginning" should take you to Chapter One, or wherever you inserted the "start" bookmark.

Check carefully through the document for errors in chapter title headings, or other glitches. If there are errors, go back to your original ebook document, fix them, and then go through the steps of saving it as a web page again into the Kindlefiles folder, etc. (Be sure to delete the old files from your Kindlefiles folder and Kindlefiles zip folder first!)

If everything is as it should be, you are finished!

## Upload Your Book Cover to Kindle

The KDP platform also allows you to upload your book cover. Amazon requires that the file be either in JPG or TIFF format, and in RGB color. The image should be a minimum of 1000 pixels on the longest side, however, Amazon recommends 2500 pixels on the longest side for better quality.

Here is Kindle's Faq for more information:

*https://kdp.amazon.com/self-publishing/
help?topicId=A2J0TRG6OPX0VM*

Amazon also provides an option to insert the cover into your document, if you have not done so already. The Faq above has a link with more details about this option. If your book already has the cover image inserted, merely uncheck the box next to "the book cover inside this book."

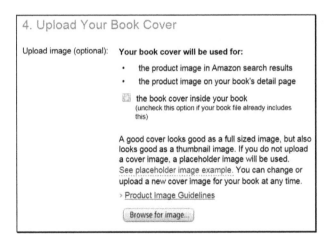

# Barnes & Noble's NOOK Format

arnes & Noble will accept an ebook submitted in Microsoft Word .doc format. They also accept .ePub uploads, and other types of formats, too. The following is a link for more information on Barnes & Noble's PubIt! program:

*http://pubit.barnesandnoble.com/pubit_app/bn?t=support#pricing_ payment_terms*

Here is the PubIt! home page:

*http://pubit.barnesandnoble.com/*

Since Barnes & Noble will accept the Microsoft Word .doc format, uploading a file to PubIt! is very easy. When you're in PubIt!'s book setup page, simply select and upload the Microsoft Word *.doc* file that you just formatted for Kindle. (Not the zip folder or web html file.) It's that simple!

Barnes & Noble's NOOK also accepts the Table of Contents generated by the Microsoft Word program, just as Kindle does. After uploading your file, I would recommend checking the links to make sure they work. Use the NOOK for PC previewer mentioned earlier in this book to check the overall formatting of your book, as well.

# Smashwords Format

Smashwords is a fantastic distributor site for ebooks. Please take a glance at Appendix E for a complete listing of the online retailers to whom they distribute.

Many people grumble about Smashwords' "Meatgrinder," and how difficult it is to make files compliant to their requirements (you are going to learn how easy it is). They also complain that the "Meatgrinder" spits out less than stellar files. I totally disagree. Your files are as good as you make them. Sure, Smashwords doesn't allow large font sizes or fancy lettering, or a few other formatting perks. However, you can still make your ebook look great.

Better yet, Smashwords' much maligned "Meatgrinder" converts your Microsoft Word document into *ten* different file formats. These files can be downloaded from the Smashwords site to readers anywhere in the world—places where Amazon and Barnes & Noble may never reach. Would you like international readers to buy your book? Just state on your website that your book is available at Smashwords, which means it is available for purchase and download *anywhere* in the world. I recently had a glowing review for one of my titles from a reader in Kenya! It is thrilling to know that everyone in the world has access to my books through Smashwords.

So, if you hear any complaints about the "Meatgrinder," take them with a grain of salt.

Now, let's get down to the nitty gritty of making your ebook file compliant to Smashwords' standards. Smashwords states that the "proper source file to upload to Smashwords is a Microsoft Word .doc file." As mentioned earlier, they do not support the .docx file.

To make your Smashwords file, you will use your Kindle .doc file once again. However, since Smashwords requires several more adjustments to the ebook file, open your Kindle file and save it as a new name. I like to include "Smashwords" (without quotes, of course) in the title, so I will remember that this file is for Smashwords alone.

Here is the link to Smashwords' home page:

*http://www.smashwords.com/*

Once again, here is a link to the Smashwords Style Guide:

*http://www.smashwords.com/books/view/52*

## Smashwords Table of Contents

As mentioned earlier, the *Smashwords Style Guide* emphatically states that the Table of Contents generated automatically by Microsoft Word should *not* be used for the files submitted to their website, since it uses field codes. Smashwords' author recommends typing the TOC by hand, and then manually creating the hyperlinked table of contents. This method will be explained shortly.

In addition, Smashwords recommends linking your TOC to an "About the Author" page and an "Other Books by this Author" page in your ebook. Both can be great marketing tools if you insert hyperlinks to your website on the pages, or links to buy your books. However, do not include affiliate links, or the file will be rejected by some ebook distributors.

### If You Already Have a Microsoft Word TOC

If you already have a Microsoft Word generated Table of Contents, you may not have to type your Table of Contents all over again by hand. You will still want to get rid of the field codes, however. Fortunately, there is an easy, two step process to do this.

First, select all of the text in your Table of Contents. Then press the keys "Ctrl + Shift + F9." Using the "Ctrl + C" keys, copy this text from your Microsoft Word document, and paste it into a simple text editor, such as Notepad. Notepad will automatically delete all formatting from the text, including the field codes.

Once the text is pasted in Notepad, select all of the text again and copy it. Paste it back into your Microsoft Word document a few lines below your old TOC. The field codes are now eliminated, and the basic text of your Table of Contents remains. If you wish to center, or otherwise format your Table of Contents with indents, now is the time to do so. When you have finished formatting your TOC, be sure to delete the old Table of Contents!

Go to the next section to learn how to hyperlink your new TOC to the chapters in your book.

### Hyperlink Table of Contents

Be sure to place the Table of Contents into your book after the front matter of your book, and before the Preface, Introduction, or Chapter One—whichever comes first. Separate it by page breaks, and then label it Table of Contents (format it with the ChapterHeading style).

If you're typing your TOC by hand, list each of the chapters to which you'd like the TOC to hyperlink. Type each chapter on a separate line. I like to center the list.

Next, you will need to place a bookmark in your document for each chapter you've included in the TOC. This is easy, and the following pictures will show you how. Start with the "Table of Contents" heading on the TOC page. Select it, and then go to *Insert, Bookmark,* and then label it "ref_toc" (without the quotes). Click "Add."

Next, go to your Chapter One heading (or Preface, Prologue; whichever section comes first) in your *text—not* on the Table of Contents page—and add a bookmark named "start" (again, without the quotes). The "start" designation tells ebook reading devices that this is the beginning text of your book.

If you've added a cover, select the cover, and name it "cover".

*Note:* The "toc," "start," and "cover" bookmarks are probably present in the file, if you formatted your Kindle .doc file as suggested in the *Kindle Format* chapter. However, Smashwords recommends that "toc" be named "ref_toc", although either will usually work.

Now, go through the document, selecting each chapter title heading and adding a bookmark to it. Be sure to choose bookmark names that make sense. For example, Chapter Two might be named "ChapterTwo" or "ch2" (no spaces).

Next, you will hyperlink the chapters listed on the Table of Contents page to the actual chapter locations. Again, this may sound complicated, but it is incredibly easy.

Select Chapter One on the TOC page, go to *Insert, Hyperlink,* and then click "Place in this Document." Under Bookmarks, you will see "start" listed. Click on "start" and then click *OK.* Now Chapter One is hyperlinked.

Next, select Chapter Two in the TOC, and repeat the same procedure. Only this time under Bookmarks you will choose "ChapterTwo" (or "ch2"). Click *OK.* Continue hyperlinking the remaining chapters listed on the TOC page, and for the cover as well, if you have included it in the TOC.

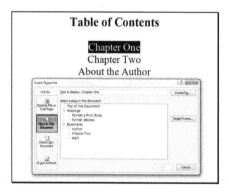

At this point, many authors choose to hyperlink the Chapters within the main document back to the Table of Contents. This is simple. Go to each chapter heading within your main document (obviously, not the chapter listing on the TOC page), select the chapter heading text, and insert a hyperlink to "ref_toc" or "toc."

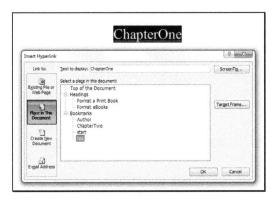

Now go to your Table of Contents and check each of your links by clicking (or "Ctrl + clicking") on them, to make sure they go where they are supposed to go. If not, fix any errors.

## Insert Smashwords' Required Text

According to Smashwords, your copyright page must include the book name, the author name, and a statement of copyright by the author. In addition, Smashwords requires that the following be placed on the copyright page:

*Published by Firstname Lastname [or PublisherName] at Smashwords*

*(or, alternatively, if you don't want to use the "Published by..." line, add the words, Smashwords Edition, on the next line. No need to do both.)*

Additional information on this subject can be found on pg. 56 of the *Smashwords Style Guide*.

## Insert Smashwords' License Notes

Insert the following text into your copyright page:

### Smashwords Edition, License Notes

*This ebook is licensed for your personal enjoyment only. This ebook may not be re-sold or given away to other people. If you would like to share this book with another person, please purchase an additional copy for each recipient. If you're reading this book and did not purchase it, or it was not purchased for your use only, then please return to Smashwords.com and purchase your own copy. Thank you for respecting the hard work of this author.*

## Delete Reference to "Printed" on Copyright Page

Smashwords does not want any reference to the book being "printed" on the copyright or title pages. This is because it is an ebook, and will not be printed. This is a simple enough fix. For example, if your printed book states "Printed in the United States of America," change it to state "Published in the United States of America."

## Smashwords eBook ISBN

As mentioned earlier, Smashwords *does* require an ISBN if you would like your book to be included in Smashwords' Premium Catalog, which includes distribution to Sony, Apple, and other online retailers. You can use your own ISBN (but again, it must be different than your print book's ISBN), or Smashwords will supply you with one of their own ISBNs. Go here to find out more:

*http://www.smashwords.com/dashboard/ISBNManager*

It is not necessary to place the ISBN on the copyright page of the Smashwords ebook edition, but if you would like to do so, now is the time to include it.

## Copyright Page Example

The following is an example of a copyright page published by Diamond Press:

Save the changes, and now your ebook is ready for upload to Smashwords! Congratulations on formatting your book for three different online retailers.

> *Tip:* If your document encounters problems with Smashwords' "Meatgrinder," please go to Appendix B for troubleshooting tips.

# Lightning Source eBooks

*J*f you have an account with Lightning Source, you may want to participate in one of their ebook distribution programs. At the time of the publication of this book, two ebook distribution programs are available through LSI: 1) the standard LSI eBook Program, and 2) the new Independent Publishers Program (IPP).

## Standard LSI eBook Program

Enrolling your books in the standard LSI eBook Program is currently free. LSI literature states that the regular fee for ebooks "is being indefinitely waived." For a list of online retailers to whom LSI distributes, please see Appendix E.

In the standard LSI eBook Program, the publisher chooses the retail price, and the publisher also chooses the discount offered to retailers. LSI currently takes 7.5% of the net price as a fulfillment fee. For example, a $10 ebook with a 25% discount means that $7.50 is the net price. Of this, LSI would take 7.5%, or $0.56; leaving $6.94 for the publisher.

LSI accepts three file formats for their ebook program: PDF for the Adobe Reader (you can also submit an .ePub), and .pdb for the Palm Reader. You need only upload the formats you currently have available. This chapter of the book will explain how to create PDF and .pdb files for LSI.

A marketing image for the standard LSI eBook Program is required, and it should be 510 x 680 pixels, 96 dpi, in JPG format, and in RGB color space.

### Independent Publishers Program (IPP)

Enrolling your books in LSI's new Independent Publishers Program provides the opportunity to distribute your ebook to a number of retailers. The current costs of joining the IPP consist of a one time market fee, and a per year storage fee per ebook. As well, a 40% discount to retailers is required, and LSI keeps a percentage of the net sale as a fulfillment fee. For more information, please contact your LSI sales representative.

If you choose to add Amazon to the distributor list, you must sign a separate agreement. Read all IPP agreements carefully for fees and discounts that you must offer to Amazon (and other IPP retail partners, as well).

The Independent Publishers Program also provides the ability to distribute your books to Barnes & Noble and the Apple iBookstore (a separate agreement is required for Apple). Contact your LSI sales representative for more information about this program, and for a complete list of all retail distribution partners. See Appendix E.

## Format PDF for LSI

LSI requires that all fonts be embedded in a PDF file for the Adobe Reader. The file also must not contain any security settings, and the file must be named *ISBN.pdf*.

Open the PDF/X-1a:2001 file that you made for your print book. Save the file as *ISBN.pdf* (for example, *9780984404445.pdf*). Do not include the .pdf extension in the name; Adobe Acrobat will provide the extension name to the file.

Unfortunately, embedding the fonts in your PDF file means that the hyperlinked Table of Contents that you created will be "unclick-able." If you would like to include "clickable" navigation in your PDF file, you will need to use Adobe Acrobat's "Bookmark" feature. For information on how to include bookmarks in your PDF document, please visit the section entitled, "Create Bookmarks in Your LITB PDF," on page 197, in *Part Four* of this book.

You will probably discover that the print version of your book has several blank pages that you might like to delete from the ebook version. Deleting them is simple. Click on the white, rectangular *Pages* icon on the left side of the screen. This will expand the *Pages* panel. Click on the little gear gadgets beneath the word "Pages" and click "Delete Pages." Delete unwanted pages from your PDF. Be sure to save your file after you are finished!

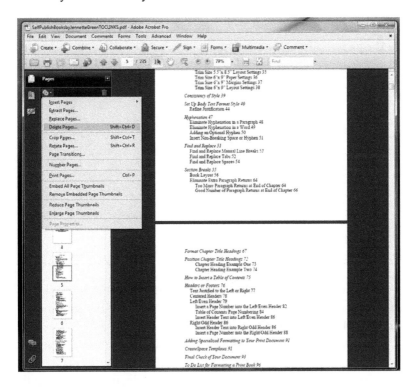

## Format PDB for LSI

A .pdb file is an ebook made for the Palm Reader for LSI. It is fairly simple to make this file, if you have downloaded Calibre, a free ebook management program. It is available here:

*http://calibre-ebook.com/*

Open Calibre and click the red "Add Books" button at the top of the screen. Select and open the html document that you made for your Kindle ebook. (Not the zip file—only the .htm file within the

Kindlefiles folder.) The following image shows what your screen will look like after you have done so.

You may notice that beneath the brown book on the far right side of the screen are the words "Formats: ZIP." Calibre has designated that your html file is a zip file.

With your new file highlighted in blue beneath "Title," as in the previous image, click the brown "Convert Books" button at the top of the screen. You will now convert your html document into a .pdb ebook.

In the dialogue box that appears, type in the book title, author name, and publisher, if you wish. Next, click the down arrow button next to "Output format" and select "PDB."

If you have included a cover image within your book, do not upload a cover image under the section entitled, "Change cover image." Conversely, if you did not include a cover image in your original Kindle ebook, now is your opportunity to include the book cover in the beginning of your .pdb ebook.

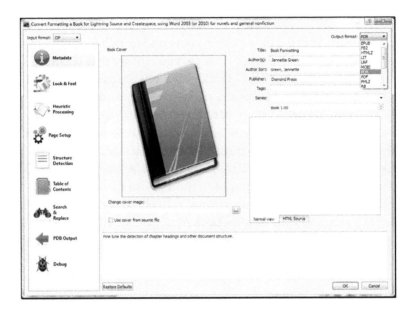

Next, in the left column, click the button that says "PDB Output." A new dialogue box will appear. In the top right portion of the box, click the down arrow button and choose "ereader." (See the following image.) Then click *OK*.

Calibre will now process the file, and you will return to the main Calibre page. After the file has been converted to .pdb format, in the right column, beneath the book image, you will see that "PDB" has been added next to the "ZIP" file. Click this blue-highlighted "PDB" link to check your .pdb book and make sure it looks as it should.

The .pdb format adds an extra line space between paragraphs. This is another reason why it is important not to add an empty paragraph return between paragraphs when you made your original ebook. If you did, you will now see a double paragraph return between each of your paragraphs in the .pdb ebook format.

If you find any problems in your .pdb ebook format, you will need to go back to your Kindle ebook Microsoft Word .doc file, and make the changes necessary. (You may want to save the file as a new name, just for the .pdb version.) Then remake the "Web, filtered html" file in Microsoft Word, and then convert the html file into a .pdb file in Calibre again.

In Windows 7, Calibre automatically saves files under Users/MyName/Calibre Library. Your .pdb file will probably be hidden somewhere in the depths of the "Unknown" file folder. You will want to find it, copy it, and then paste your new .pdb file into the eBook folder you made for your book. That way all of your ebook files will be together, and will be easy to find when you are ready to upload them to the different distributor platforms.

Name your .pdb file *ISBN.pdb* (of course, do not add the .pdb extension—Calibre has already done this).

Please also note that the .pdb file that Calibre makes is unencrypted. When you upload it to LSI, be sure to choose the "unencrypted" option, if it is available, or else your LSI ebook technician will contact you with the news that your file contains an error.

## Apple iBookstore

LSI will also distribute ebooks to Apple's iBookstore, but to enroll in this program, you must sign an additional agreement with LSI. Read the fine print carefully for any exclusivity clauses, in which you might be required to agree to solely use LSI for uploading all of your ebooks to Apple now, and in the future. An .ePub file that passes the epubcheck at ePub Validator is required.

ePub Validator (for LSI and iBookstore):
*http://validator.idpf.org*

For additional information about advanced ebook formatting, please visit Appendix C.

# To Do List for Formatting an eBook

1. Make sure your Microsoft Word document has been saved as a .doc file. (Not a .docx file.) Use a different file name for your ebook file. If you'd like, save it in a separate folder than where your print document is stored, so that you can keep the ebook files separate.
2. Delete optional hyphens and manually adjusted character spacing.
3. Replace specialized scene break symbols with asterisks
4. Delete mirror margins, headers, footers and page numbers
5. Make sure that "line spacing" is set to "single" in the Paragraph dialogue box.
6. Replace section breaks with page breaks
7. Delete extra paragraph returns (no more than four consecutive paragraph returns anywhere in the ebook)
8. Review the additional rules and recommendations
9. Reduce font sizes of chapter headings and titles to 14 pt. (16 pt., if you're feeling daring)
10. Insert a cover image into your ebook, if desired
11. Turn off page numbers in automatically generated Table of Contents
12. Delete the print ISBN from the ebook copyright page
13. Convert your Microsoft Word file to Kindle format
14. Upload the Kindle zip folder to the KDP Platform
15. Upload the ebook Microsoft Word .doc to Barnes and Noble's PubIt! platform
16. Save your ebook .doc as a new name for Smashwords. Include Smashwords' required text, license notes, and delete reference to "printed" on the copyright page.

17. Create and hyperlink a Table of Contents for your Smash-words ebook
18. Upload to Smashwords

*3*

# Prepare Your Cover

## Overview

*N*ow it's time to prepare your cover image for Lightning Source and CreateSpace. The best tools to use are Adobe Photoshop and Adobe Acrobat Pro. Some publishers and authors use Scribus, which is a free program available online, but this book does not cover the use of Scribus. (Please see Appendix E for a helpful link.)

I use Adobe Photoshop CS5 and Adobe Acrobat Pro 9. The commands in earlier or later versions should be similar. Please note that other image software programs can be used to create your cover; however, if your file will be uploaded to LSI, then Adobe Photoshop or Scribus will be needed to finish it. More on this later.

Although this section will cover the requirements necessary to make cover files compliant with the standards of both LSI and CS, I will primarily address LSI's requirements, as they are more stringent. If your cover meets LSI's standards, it will meet CS's standards, as well.

In this section of the book, the terms CMYK color and RGB color will be used. Please note that these are two different color spaces. Although I will not go into all of the fine points of the two color profiles, suffice it to say that CMYK colors are used for print publications, and RGB colors are used for the internet, color monitors, and ebooks.

Since this section is about printing covers for physical books, we will discuss ways to achieve the best CMYK color for your cover files.

Most image programs, especially the free versions, such as Gimp, use RGB color. Your image program may or may not be able to convert RGB colors into the CMYK colors required for printing. It is certainly possible to build your cover in one of these free programs. If you are making a cover for CreateSpace, that program may be all you need. Please see the next section, which is entitled, "A Note About CreateSpace Covers," for more information.

However, although you can certainly build your cover in a low-priced image program, if you will be submitting your cover to LSI, you need to be aware that they enforce a 240% ink limits requirement on all cover files. That means that your darkest colors can be a maximum of 240% ink saturation. This is a problem, as black is typically 300%, and other dark colors present similar issues.

As a result, while you definitely can build your cover in a free or low-priced image program, you will eventually need to convert your file to LSI's 240% ink percentage requirements. As of the publication of this book, the only programs I know that will do this conversion are Adobe Photoshop, and Scribus. So, you will need to use Scribus, or a friend's Adobe Photoshop program to apply the 240% ink limits to your file, or else you will need to hire someone (such as myself, or another freelancer) to do the work for you. Diamond Press currently charges $35 to convert a cover file. You may find a different, competitive price from a freelancer online.

## A Note About CreateSpace Covers

If you would like to create a cover file for CreateSpace, as mentioned before, it is certainly possible to do so with GIMP (a free, open source image program available online), or another image software program of your choice. Although your image program may not provide the ability to convert your images to CMYK color, a work-around to create a CMYK cover PDF is possible.

First, read this entire *Part Three,* "Prepare Your Cover," portion of the book in order to familiarize yourself with the template and the techniques necessary to create a cover that will pass CreateSpace standards. Of particular importance is to ensure that your image is the correct dpi, and placed properly on the CreateSpace template.

After you have made sure that your cover is the correct dpi and placed on the appropriate template, save it as a flattened (all layers flattened into one layer) TIFF file. Open the file in Adobe Acrobat. Next, go to the section entitled, "Save Cover as a PostScript File," which is located on page 187.

When you make a PostScript file, and then afterward process the file using the PDF/X-1a:2001 settings in Acrobat Distiller, the RGB colors will change into CMYK colors. Make no mistake, however, this method will not work for LSI, because black will be converted to 300% ink saturation, which is prohibited by LSI. As mentioned before, LSI's maximum ink limit is 240%. CreateSpace does not have this requirement. Please read on to learn more about preparing your cover for CreateSpace.

## Save Your Cover Image as a New File Name

Let's begin work on your file. Since you will be making changes to your cover image in the following sections, it is best to preserve your original file. Open the original file, and "save as" a new file name—I like to add "CMYK" (without quotes) to the file name, so I can distinguish it from the original (for example, *MyCoverCMYK*). Now you have a new file to work from, and the original will remain untouched.

# Cover Resolution

The resolution of your cover image must be 300 dpi for both LSI and CS. As mentioned in previous parts of this book, I will use the terms "dpi" (dots per inch) and "ppi" (pixels per inch) interchangeably. Although they are not technically the same thing, they are close enough for our purposes.

To check the resolution of your cover, open your image file in Adobe Photoshop. Go to *Image* and click *Image Size*. In the dialogue box that appears, look at the resolution of your image. The "Resolution" box should say "300."

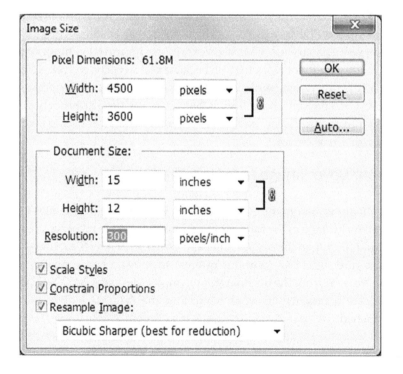

If it does not say "300," you have some work to do. If the resolution is close to "300," you may be able to adjust the resolution from the *Image Size* dialogue box.

Some experts recommend using the "Bicubic Sharper (best for reduction)" setting to adjust the image resolution. They recommend using this setting whether you plan to increase or reduce the size of the image.

Make the adjustment necessary in the "Resolution" box, but make certain the "Document Size" of the image does not change. It should not, if the checked box settings portrayed in the previous image are used. However, the "Pixel Dimensions" will change. That is fine.

If the resolution of your image is more than 10% less than 300 dpi (and this is just a rough estimate), you may not want to adjust the resolution in this dialogue box, for the quality of the image will noticeably downgrade. If you want to try, anyway, one expert recommends increasing the resolution by 5–10% at a time.

Use the recommended settings listed in the previous paragraph. Then check your image quality in the main screen. I like to zoom in to at least 200% and see how sharp and clear the images and text look. Are the details sharp and clear? Or are they fuzzy?

The following image is a screen shot of back cover text that was enlarged 200%. The letters are crisp, with sharp, clean edges. The text for this book printed very well at LSI.

Should Anya accept
Or is he a madman, v
brink of destruction?

If you are not happy with the quality of the image you see, you may need to go back to your original images and reconstruct the cover. This is certainly a worst case scenario. Please make certain the images you add to the cover are 300 dpi. In addition, it may be helpful to reconstruct the cover on LSI or CS's specific cover template for your book. Go to Appendix D to learn how to construct your cover image on a template. Be certain to read the following sections first, however.

# The Cover Template

*I*f your image resolution is correct, it is time to download the template for your book from either Lightning Source or CreateSpace.

## Download Cover Template from Lightning Source

The cover generator for LSI can be found on a link on their main page. (You do not have to be logged in to access it.) Go to:

*http://www.lightningsource.com/*

Click on *File Creation* and then *Cover Template Generator*. The following is a clip of the screen that you will see next.

| | |
|---|---|
| 13-digit ISBN (with dashes): | [_____]  Click here to convert your 10-digit ISBN to |
| Publisher Reference Number: | [_____] |
| Interior Type: | ⦿ Black & White  ○ Premium Color  ○ Standard Color |
| Binding Type: | ⦿ Case Laminate  ○ Cloth Bound  ○ Perfect Bound  ○ Saddle |
| Paper Type: | ⦿ Creme  ○ White |
| Laminate Type: | ⦿ Gloss  ○ Matte  (Laminate type does not alter template specs) |
| Book Type: | [_____] |
| Page Count: | [_____] |
| File Type to Return: | [ InDesign CS3 and newer ⬍ ] |
| Email Address: | [_____] |
| Retype Email Address: | [_____] |

Optional Information:

| | |
|---|---|
| Price (including decimal): | [_____]  Currency: [ US Dollars ⬍ ] |
| Price in Bar Code: | [ No ⬍ ] |

Fill out the required fields. If your book interior will be black and white (no color images inside the book), you will choose "Content Type: B&W." Choose the paper color you would like for your book. I like to use "Creme" for fiction, and either "Creme" or "White" for nonfiction. "Laminate Type" refers to the cover. Do you want it to look glossy, or would you prefer it to have a matte finish? Most books published have the "Gloss" finish.

Next, choose your book type. Click the down arrow at the far end of the "Book Type" box. A list of book trim sizes and binding options will appear. Find the trim size for your book, and make sure that "Perfect Bound" is listed on the same line if you plan to publish a paperback book. If you will publish a hardback, choose the appropriate options for your book. For illustration purposes, the template for a perfect bound book will be used in this manual.

| Book Type: | ▼ |
|---|---|
| Page Count: | B&W 5 x 8 in or 203 x 127 mm Perfect Bound on Creme w/Gloss Lam |
| pe to Return: | B&W 5.250 x 8.000 in or 203 x 133mm Perfect Bound on Creme w/Gloss Lam |
| nail Address: | B&W 5.5 x 8.5 in or 216 x 140 mm (Demy 8vo) Blue Cloth w/Jacket on Creme w/Gloss Lam |
| | B&W 5.5 x 8.5 in or 216 x 140 mm (Demy 8vo) Case Laminate on Creme w/Gloss Lam |
| nail Address: | B&W 5.5 x 8.5 in or 216 x 140 mm (Demy 8vo) Gray Cloth w/Jacket on Creme w/Gloss Lam |
| | B&W 5.5 x 8.5 in or 216 x 140 mm (Demy 8vo) Perfect Bound on Creme w/Gloss Lam |
| | B&W 5.83 x 8.27 in or 210 x 148 mm (A5) Perfect Bound on Creme w/Gloss Lam |
| | B&W 6 x 9 in or 229 x 152 mm Blue Cloth w/Jacket on Creme w/Gloss Lam |
| ing decimal): | B&W 6 x 9 in or 229 x 152 mm Case Laminate on Creme w/Gloss Lam |
| | B&W 6 x 9 in or 229 x 152 mm Gray Cloth w/Jacket on Creme w/Gloss Lam |
| in Bar Code: | B&W 6 x 9 in or 229 x 152 mm Perfect Bound on Creme w/Gloss Lam |

Next, enter the *total* number of pages in your book, including the front matter. If your book has an odd number of pages, such as 197 pages, round up to the next even number. In this example, you would type 198 in the "Page Count" box.

Select the "File Type to Return." I choose PDF, although EPS would work just as well for Adobe Photoshop. The instructions in this book will be directed toward working with the PDF file.

Type in your email address, as required, and the retail price for your book. Select the currency, and then choose if you would like the price included in the ISBN bar code. Major publishers include the price in the ISBN bar code, but many small publishers choose not to do so. Here is why: If a small publisher later decides to change the price of a book, a whole new cover file, with the new, correct price, will need to be formatted and uploaded to LSI. LSI may charge as much as $40 for processing this new, revised file.

> *Tip:* If you plan to submit your book to Barnes & Noble's Small Press department, please note that they require both the ISBN and the price to appear on the back cover of the book. For more information, please visit:
>
> *http://www.barnesandnobleinc.com/for_authors/how_to_work_wit h_bn/how_to_work_with_bn.html*

## Download Cover Template from CreateSpace

The cover template generator for CreateSpace can be located at the following link:

*https://www.createspace.com/Help/Book/Artwork.do*

Input the information for your book. The following is a portion of CS's template generator page, with sample requirements included.

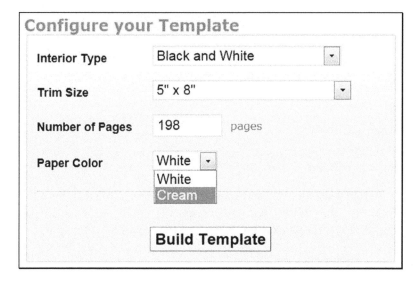

Click "Build Template," and the next web page will provide a download link entitled, "Click here to begin Download." The download zip file contains both a PNG and a PDF template. Unzip it in your computer. (To unzip a file in Microsoft Windows 7, right click on the zip file, and then choose "Extract all.") We will work with the PDF template.

## Open and Name PDF Cover Template

In Photoshop, open your cover template PDF file that you have just downloaded from either LSI or CS. Go to *File, Open,* select the PDF cover template, and click "Open."

The following image shows the next dialogue box that will appear. Choose "Mode: CMYK" as the color, and make certain "300" is in the "Resolution" box. Click *OK*.

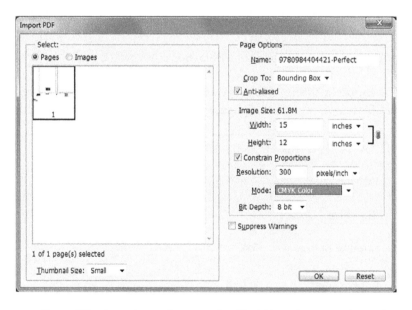

Go to *File, Save As,* and name the file *ISBN_CMYK* (where the ISBN is the ISBN for your specific book (for example, *9780984404421_CMYK*)), and save it in PSD format.

## Crop the ISBN Bar Code

If you are using the CreateSpace template, you will notice that an ISBN bar code is not included in the template, although the space where it is to be placed is clearly labeled. CreateSpace will place the ISBN bar code on your cover for you. (So will LSI, for that matter.) If you would rather place the ISBN bar code on the back cover your-self, either generate a cover template from LSI and crop out the bar code, as described in the following paragraphs, or find a bar code generator online that will produce the bar code for you. Two such sites are (choose the ISBN option for the second site):

*http://www.tux.org/~milgram/bookland/indexUsual.html*

*http://www.terryburton.co.uk/barcodewriter/generator/*

As mentioned, Lightning Source, like CreateSpace, will place the ISBN bar code on your back cover for you. If you would prefer to take advantage of this option, simply leave the space designated for the bar code free of any important text or graphics. They will then place the ISBN in that spot.

I prefer to place the ISBN bar code on the back cover myself. This way, I have more control over the final, aesthetic design of the book. If you would like to do the same, it is simple enough to do. Here's how:

First, you'll need to crop out the ISBN bar code from the cover template and save it as a separate file. Here's why: The ISBN bar code present on the template is formatted exactly as LSI requires it to be—300 dpi, and 100% registration black ink. It is important to preserve these qualities. As a result, the cropped ISBN bar code will be the last image you place on the file before you convert the cover to PDF format for LSI.

At the moment, you may see an image that looks like the picture on the following page.

## *LSI Template*

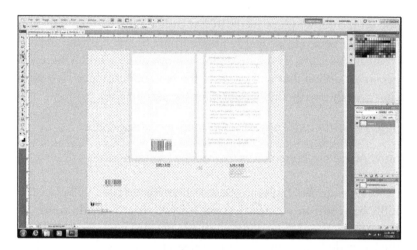

Zoom in 200%. Using the crop tool, select and crop the ISBN bar code. It is selected in the next image, and cropped in the following picture.

Go to *File,* and choose *Save As.* In the next dialogue box, under "Save Options," be certain to check the box "As a Copy." This will preserve your original cover template PSD file. Save it as *ISBN-ISBN* (in our example, the file name would be *9780984404421-ISBN*). Save it as either a TIFF (on the dialogue box for TIFF options, choose "LZW" for best "Image Compression" quality) or a PSD file.

> Note: The TIFF "LZW" is a lossless compression format. This means that the quality of your image remains the same, bit for bit, as the original file.

To return your cover template file to the way it was before you cropped out the ISBN bar code, go to your *History* panel. (In Photoshop, go to *Window,* and select *History.*) Click the line that says "Open." This will return your file to the original settings it had when you first opened the file. (You might also want to return the Zoom to 25%, so you can see the whole cover template again.)

*History Panel Enlarged on LSI Template*

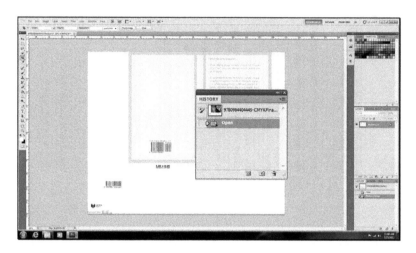

## Flatten the Cover Template

I prefer to work with a flattened template, for it makes the markings on the template easier to see. The transparent template will turn white after it is flattened.

Just in case you've never heard the term "flatten" before, this is what it means: A typical file is made up of different layers. It might have text layers, for example, image layers, and so on. Flattening a file squishes all of the text, images, etc., into one, flat as a pancake image. After it is flattened, you will no longer be able to edit any of the individual layers. So, if you have a PSD or TIFF file with a number of layers in it, be certain to save it as another file name after you flatten it. This will allow you to keep your original, layered file, in case you need to make changes to it later.

By the way, both Photoshop PSD files and ordinary TIFF files are capable of making layered files. If you do not have access to Photoshop, you can build your cover using the TIFF file format in the image program of your choice.

Back to the subject at hand. We want to flatten this template file, so that the transparent layer turns white. In actuality, no important layers will be lost in this case. To flatten the template, go to the *Layers* panel (located in the right panel of the following image), right-click the single layer that is visible, and select "Flatten Image."

## *Transparent Cover Template*

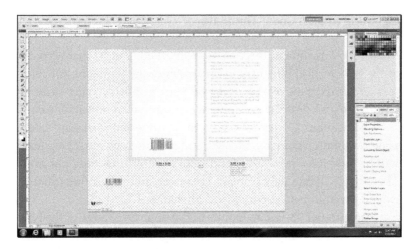

## *Flattened Cover Template*

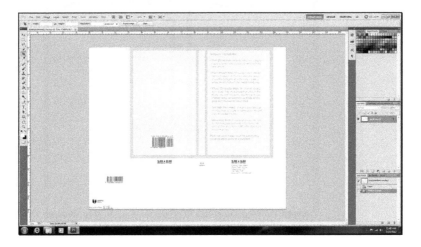

## Cover Template Components

Let's take a look at the PDF template for your book. First, we'll look at the LSI PDF template. Next, we'll look at the CS template.

### Lightning Source Cover Template

In the following image, three areas are marked. The "1" arrows point to the two vertical blue bars in the center of the template. All spine text and important images, such as your publisher logo, must fit within the pink "safe" area, and not cross into the vertical blue bars.

The number "2" arrow points to the inner edge of the "safety zone." All important text, images, and the bar code must be placed within the pink "safe" area, and not cross into the blue bar area. Then they will be safely printed. However, all backgrounds should extend through both the pink and blue areas.

The number "3" arrow points to the outermost edge of the blue bars of the book template. The cover image must extend to the edge of these blue bars, but not cross into the white area of the template.

Since you will be placing your cover on top of LSI's template, those "safety" bar lines will be covered up. An excellent way to mark those blue bars is to align guides directly over top of them. These guides are always on the "top" layer, so they remain visible at all times, even when the template is covered. These guide lines do not print.

First, make sure the Ruler is turned on in Photoshop (*View, Rulers*). Click in the left, vertical ruler and drag out a vertical guide. Place it on the innermost edge of one of the blue bars in the spine area, delineated by the number "1" in the previous image. Drag out another line for the other side of the spine. I highly recommend placing guides along all of the edges of the blue safety bars on the template. Then, when you place your cover image on the template, you will still know where the safety lines are located.

When you place your cover on the template, make sure no text crosses over into any of the blue safety bars. Otherwise, LSI will reject the cover. Let's prevent that from happening!

The following image shows the LSI template with guides in place. The black guide lines correspond to the blue bars on the template.

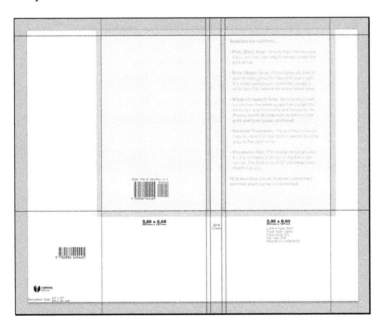

The following is an example of a correctly positioned cover on an LSI template. Please note the placement of the text and images on the front and back covers. It is important to position these elements so that they look balanced on the page between the vertical (and horizontal) safety lines.

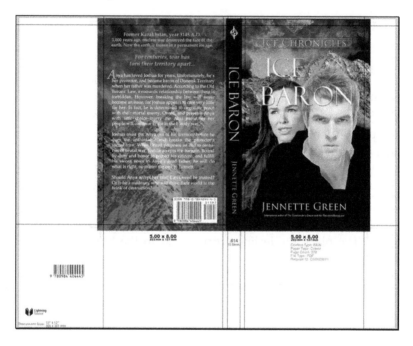

When you place text or images on your cover, always be aware that the outer edges of your book cover will be trimmed away when your book is manufactured. Account for this when you design your cover.

The following image is a close-up of the spine area. The color of the guides have been switched to light blue, so that you can see them better.

As mentioned, the light blue, vertical guide lines in the center of the image correspond to the "safety" pink zone within the spine area. Also note that the spine text and image are within the guides.

You may wish to align the outer edges of your spine with the fold marks. In the previous image, the solid black background color of the spine extends to the fold marks. (Fold marks are not marked with guidelines in this image.) Please note that important text and images, however, cannot extend to the fold lines. They must stay within the pink safety zones. See the following image for an example of how to mark the fold lines with guides.

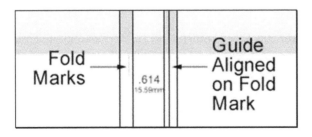

The next image is zoomed in on the bottom left corner of the cover image. Notice how the cover extends to, but does not overlap the blue border of the template. No images cross into the white area of the template.

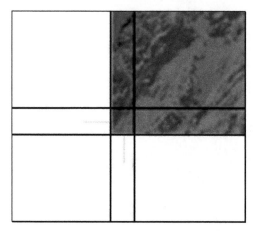

If you are working with LSI's old template, please visit the following link for more information:

*http://www.formatabook.com/book-formatting/old-lightning-source-cover-template/*

## CreateSpace Cover Template

The following image is a CreateSpace cover template. Although it looks considerably different than the LSI template, they contain the same elements.

The black-dashed lines around the outside edges indicate the book trim area. The vertical blue-dotted lines in the center indicate the spine area.

The white (or checkered/transparent area in the following image) is the "live" area. All text and images placed in this area will be printed.

The peach/pink colored, thicker lines indicate the bleed area. (These peach lines cover the black-dashed trim lines on the outside edges, and also the inner, vertical, blue-dotted spine lines.) According to CreateSpace documentation, your cover image must "extend to the outside edge" of the template's peach zone. However, text and other important details should not be placed within this area, for they will not print.

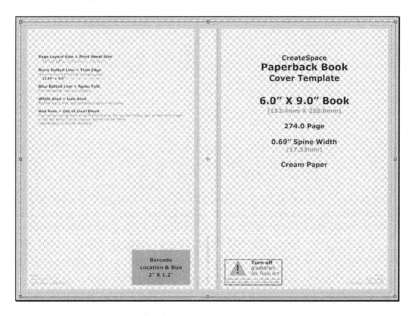

As mentioned in the LSI cover template section, you might want to place guides on your template so that you will be sure to keep your spine text within the "safety" blue-dotted (and peach/pink) vertical spine lines. Align your guides along the inner edges of the peach vertical lines in the spine area. Make sure your spine text and spine images do not cross into the peach area. In addition, be sure to draw guides for the other peach/safety areas, as well. It is important that your text and important images do not cross over into those safety zones, or the file may be rejected.

The following image shows the CreateSpace template with guides in place. The black guide lines correspond to the thick peach safety lines on the template. The ISBN area is not marked off in this image. You may wish to mark it off on your template, however.

As mentioned in the LSI section, the guide lines do not print.

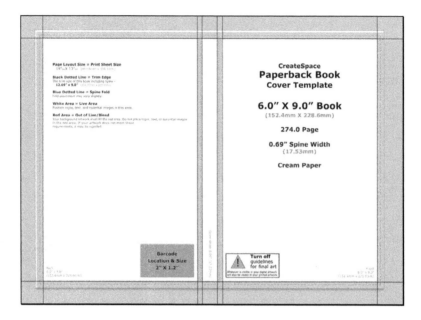

CreateSpace recommends that you put no text or important images over the rectangular bar code area. Instead, they recommend that it be filled with your background image or design.

One final note on cover positioning—as mentioned in the previous section for LSI covers, keep in mind that the outer edges of the book cover will be trimmed off when it is manufactured. As a result, make sure your text and images are balanced on the page between the vertical (and horizontal) safety guide lines.

CreateSpace also recommends that you turn off the guide layer (the instructions, dotted lines, etc.) before submitting the file. However, if you cannot do so, simply make sure your cover image completely covers all elements of the guide, so that none of guide areas of the CS template show through. Again, remember that CreateSpace requires that the cover image extend to the outside edges of the template's peach zones.

More information can be found on the cover template generator page at CreateSpace:

*https://www.createspace.com/Help/Book/Artwork.do*

# Place Your Cover Image on the Template

*P*reviously, you checked to make sure that your cover image was the required 300 dpi. Now it is time to make sure that your cover is the right size for the template. If it is not, you will need to make adjustments.

Open your template, if it is not already open. Using the Photoshop *Place* command (*File, Place*), select your cover image and place it on your template. Once it's positioned where you want it to be, hit the enter key, and it will become a separate layer in the *Layers* panel. Make sure the cover layer is the top-most layer on the template.

Now, check the outer edges of the cover image. Do they extend to, but not completely cover the outermost, blue-dotted lines (or, on the CS template, completely cover the black-dashed lines and thicker peach lines outlining the template)? It may help to zoom in 200% to fine tune the placement of the cover on the template.

If it does not exactly fit, it may be possible to resize the image so it does. (Here is one way to do so: Select the image with the arrow/pointer tool. Then go to an outer corner of the image and press Shift as you drag the box either in (to make the image smaller) or out (to enlarge the image).

However, if the image is quite a bit smaller than the template, you may need to go back and reconstruct the cover all over again. Appendix D explains how to do this. Images that are increased by a large percentage may pixelate and lose image quality. If you do increase the image size, check the image quality by zooming in to at least 200% and inspect the quality of the text. Refer back to the chapter entitled, "Cover Resolution," on page 146, for more information.

If, after you've resized the cover image, and it is still too tall vertically, or too wide horizontally, you will need to crop the image so that it fits properly. Please read Appendix D for further instructions.

When your image is the right size, and once more placed on the original PSD cover template (be sure to first delete any old cover layers that you might have previously placed in the file), again check the outer edges to make sure they are properly aligned, as described earlier—either along the blue-dotted lines (LSI) or exactly covering the outside edge of the peach lines (CS).

Also, make sure that your spine text and spine images, as well as *all* important text and images fall within the guide lines you previously set in place. Both LSI and CS are very particular about the text and images falling within those safety lines, so please be careful here. Otherwise, your file will most likely be rejected.

As mentioned in the previous sections, make sure your cover text and images look balanced on the page between the vertical and horizontal safety guide lines.

If you need to reconstruct your cover from scratch, please go to Appendix D.

# Convert Your Cover to CMYK Color

Both Lightning Source and CreateSpace covers must be converted to CMYK color.

## CreateSpace Cover and Template

At this point, the CreateSpace cover is placed on the template and almost ready to go. To make sure that your entire cover is converted to the CMYK color space, simply go to *Edit, Convert to Profile,* and in the "Profile" area, choose "Working CMYK - U.S. Web Coated (SWOP) v2." Click *OK.*

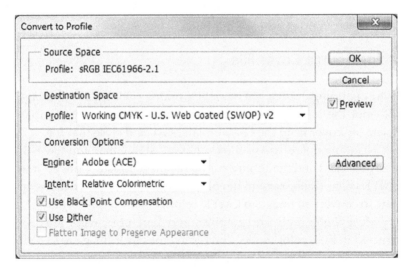

Next, go to *Edit, Assign Profile,* and select the option "Working CMYK - U.S. Web Coated (SWOP) v2." Click *OK.*

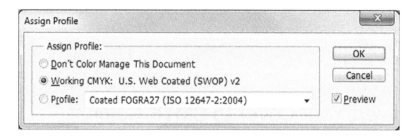

Next, if you would like to place the ISBN bar code on the back cover, do so now. Be sure that it is placed within the back cover safety lines (it does not have to be placed in the exact spot that CS designated for the bar code, however).

Now save the file as *ISBN_cov* (the ISBN is the specific ISBN for your book, with no dashes, such as *9780984404445_cov*). Next, go to the chapter entitled, "Create Your Cover PDF," which is located on page 183.

Alternately, if you do not have the Adobe Photoshop program, you could save your file as a flattened TIFF file, and then open it in Adobe Acrobat Pro. Next, go to the section entitled, "Save Cover as a PostScript File," which is located on page 187, within the "Create Your Cover PDF" chapter of this book.

## Lightning Source Cover File

With Lightning Source, we are still working with the cover image file—not the template—at this point. Just to keep things simple, delete the cover from the LSI template, save and close that file.

Next, open your cover file (*MyCoverCMYK*), that you have already checked and made sure *exactly* fits the template. Convert it to CMYK color. (Refer back to the previous section for instructions on how to convert an image to CMYK color.)

Most photographs and graphics (and therefore, covers) are constructed in RGB color mode. Converting the cover image to CMYK color mode will produce a color change, because the two color spaces are very different. While much could be said on this subject, it will not change the basic fact that CMYK colors will never exactly match RGB colors. It is generally best to accept the small difference in color.

While you're here, save a copy of your file as *MyCoverCMYK2*. Now you have two files that are identical. You will use them in the next chapter.

# Adjust Cover Ink Percentages (LSI Only)

*A*ll covers submitted to Lightning Source must be in CMYK color and meet LSI's maximum 240% ink limit. (CreateSpace covers do not need to be adjusted for ink percentages.) This means that while the image resolution must be 300 dpi, the ink percentage (or ink saturation) can only be a maximum of 240%. This is always a problem, for the default ink percentage for black is 300%. Black, and the other dark colors in your cover, must be reduced in ink saturation to 240%.

Photoshop makes it simple to reduce the ink percentage saturation. While the procedure may be easy, the results are less than stellar. When a color's ink percentage is reduced this drastically, color changes take place in the cover. Black may turn gray. Blue may turn purple, orange may look brown, and so on. How do you prevent this from happening?

Several methods are available to compensate for the color shift that occurs when an image is converted to 240% ink percentages.

## Check the Ink Percentages in Your Cover Image

Now it's time to check the ink percentages in your cover image. Use the *MyCoverCMYK* file that you just made.

Go to *Window*, and click *Info*. The *Info* panel will appear. In the far right corner of the *Info* panel is a tiny arrow down button next to four little straight lines. Click on the down arrow, and the "Info Panel Options" dialogue box will appear. Under "Second Color Readout" choose "Mode: Total Ink." Click *OK*. Now when you move your cursor over your image, the total ink for that exact spot will show up in the *Info* panel. Let's give it a try.

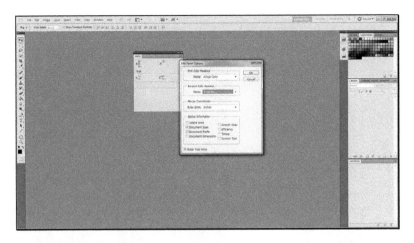

*A Close Up of the Previous Image*

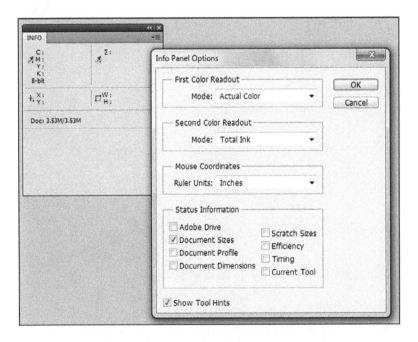

In the following picture, I've placed my cursor over the black in the man's jacket. If you read the ink readout on the right side of the *Info* panel, you will see that it reads "300%." This is the total ink percentage for that bit of the picture.

Try this with your image. Go to the darkest portion first. Does it read a number higher than 240%? If so, you will need to go to the next step. If not, check other areas of the picture. If no colors go over the 240% ink limits, and the colors look good, then you are finished with this section. Go to the "Create Your Cover PDF" chapter.

## Method One: Apply ICC  Profiles

Method One may be the only procedure you will need to use to adjust the ink percentages. In the past, I went round and round, trying to adjust for the color changes that occurred when the 240% ink limits were applied to a cover. It was a long and tedious process, but the colors always turned out well in the end.

More recently, I have been following Aaron Shepard's advice to first apply the HP Indigo ICC profile to the file, and then apply the 240% Ink Percentage ICC profile to the file. After that, I adjust the color balance, and the file is good to go. As I said, this usually works, but not always. Other methods will be listed in later sections.

A big thank you to Aaron Shepard for taking the time to provide these color profiles to all POD publishers! His website is a source of valuable information, and I own all of his POD books—these are highly recommended by this author.

Aaron Shepard's website:
*http://www.newselfpublishing.com/*

Download zip file for HP Indigo Profile:
*http://www.newselfpublishing.com/HPIndigo.zip*

Download zip file for LSI Ink Percentage Limits:
*http://www.newselfpublishing.com/TotalInkLimit.zip*

These ICC files will be used by Photoshop to convert your images to the proper color profiles and ink percentages required by LSI. Unzip the files on your computer. Copy and paste the ICC profiles into the following location (if your computer gives you a warning, just ignore it and continue on—you will not be changing anything; you'll just be adding two extra files to the folder):

*Windows® Operating Systems:*
NT, 2000, XP, Vista, Win 7

*ICC File Folder Location:*
Windows > System32 > Spool > Drivers > Color

Paste the two ICC profiles into the "Color" folder.

*Note:* If you would prefer not to download or place these two ICC profiles on your computer, skip the "Apply HP Indigo Profile to Cover" section, and go directly to the "Manually Adjust to 240% Ink Limits" section. Alternate instructions are given on page 177 so that you can manually adjust the ink percentages within the Adobe Photoshop program.

Now you're ready to move on to the next step. In Photoshop, open the two identical cover files that you have made (*My-CoverCMYK* and *MyCoverCMYK2*). Close all other files that might be open.

*Tip:* Make sure your image is flattened before you apply the ICC profiles, or else the profiles may not work properly.

You will be applying the color changes to the CMYK2 file. At the same time, you will want to be able to see your original, CMYK file. This way, you can see the color changes that take place, and then later adjust the colors in the CMYK2 file to match the originals.

In order to see the images side by side, look for the "Arrange Documents" icon, located at the top of the Photoshop screen (see the following image). Click the little down arrow and select the option which will allow you to see two images side by side.

*Two Images Side by Side*

**Apply HP Indigo Profile to Cover**

Click in the window which displays *MyCoverCMYK2*, to make it active. Next, you will convert the image to the HP Indigo ICC profile. Go to *Edit, Convert to Profile*. Click the down arrow next to the profile box.

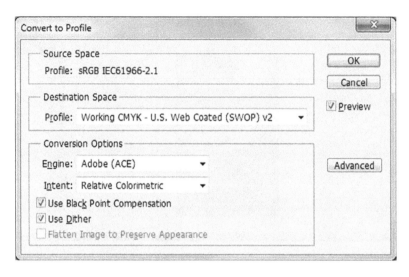

Select "HP Indigo 5000..." It is near the bottom of the list. While you're there, notice the profile entitled, "Lightning Source Cover CMYK (238%)" that is just below it. You will use this profile shortly. Click *OK*.

Next, you will need to assign a profile to the image. Go to *Edit, Assign Profile,* and select the option "Working CMYK - U.S. Web Coated (SWOP) v2." Click *OK*.

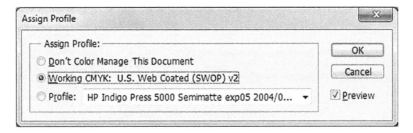

*Tip:* Sometimes the HP Indigo profile changes the colors so drastically that the colors can never be adjusted to look like they were originally. I have found bright purple to be one of these problem colors. I'm sure there are others. If your cover colors changed drastically in this step, you may need to undo the conversion to the HP profile (in the *History* panel, click on the step prior to converting the cover to the HP profile). Instead, simply apply the LSI 240% ink limits to the cover. This step is covered in the next section.

## Apply LSI 240% Ink Limits to Cover

Now, you will convert your cover image to LSI's 240% ink limits. Make sure your *MyCoverCMYK2* window is active (you must apply the HP Indigo profile and the LSI Ink Limits profile to the same image).

Go to *Edit, Convert to Profile,* and this time choose the "Lightning Source Cover CMYK (238%)" profile. Click *OK.*

*Note:* The "Lightning Source Cover CMYK (238%)" profile converts your colors to 238% ink saturation. This 2% reduction from the total LSI ink limit of 240% allows for variations in color conversion so that the total, final limits do not exceed 240%.

## Manually Adjust to 240% Ink Limits

If you chose not to download the ICC profiles to your computer, it is certainly possible to manually adjust the ink percentages within the Photoshop program. Go to *Edit, Convert to Profile,* and choose "Custom CMYK." It is located near the top of the pull down menu. A warning box may come up. Click *OK.* In the "Custom CMYK" dialogue box change "Dot gain" to "25%." Change "Total Ink Limit" to "238," as shown in the following image. Click *OK.*

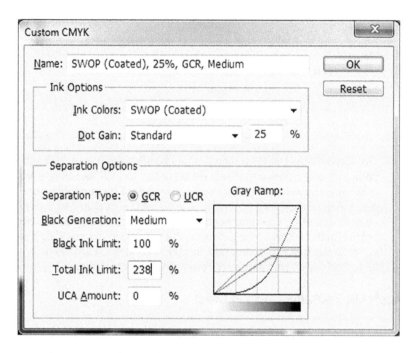

Next, assign a profile to the image. Go to *Edit, Assign Profile,* and select the option "Working CMYK - U.S. Web Coated (SWOP) v2." Click *OK*.

Check the ink percentages in your *MyCoverCMYK2* image file. The darkest spot should be under 240%. If it is not, check to make sure the file is flattened. If it is not, you will need to flatten it and repeat this step.

### Adjust the Cover Colors

Look at the two images that appear side by side in your window (*MyCoverCMYK* and *MyCoverCMYK2*). The image (*MyCoverCMYK2*), to which you applied the two ICC profiles, probably looks much different than your original image (*MyCoverCMYK*). Now is the time to adjust for the difference, and to try to make the CMYK2 image come as close as possible to the original CMYK image—or until you are happy with it.

The first thing to try is to adjust the color balance. Go to *Image, Adjustments,* "Color Balance." The following dialogue box will appear.

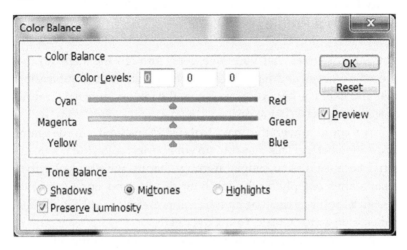

Make sure the "Preview" button is checked. Compare the two images (CMYK and CMYK2) as you adjust the three different sliders. Adjust the color until you find a balance that looks as close as possible to your original image. Jot down the numbers listed in the "Color Levels" boxes. You may want to refer to them later. Click *OK.*

If you are happy with how your cover image looks now, check the dark part of the cover again in the *Info* panel. Are the darkest colors still below 240%? If not, go to "Method Two." If they are, then go to the chapter entitled, "Create Your Cover PDF," on page 183.

If you are still not happy with the colors in your CMYK2 file, you can try to adjust other color factors. Among these (both are accessed via *Image, Adjustments*) are "Brightness/Contrast," and "Hue/Saturation." Again, when you find a color adjustment that you like, note down the color adjustment method (Color Balance, etc.), and the numbers that produced the output you like. I find I often refer back to these numbers, especially when I am trying to fine-tune the colors of a cover.

When you are happy with the colors, again check the ink percentages in the "Info" panel. Are the darkest colors still below 240%?

If not, go to "Method Two." If they are, then go to the chapter entitled, "Create Your Cover PDF," on page 183.

## Method Two: Apply Color Changes to Cover *Before* Converting to a Profile

This step assumes that you have gone through the steps on the preceding pages and have found a color adjustment combination that you like. The only problem is that the ink percentages are now *over* 240% again. What to do?

You could convert the image to the 238% ink limits profile again, as detailed before. This may foul up your perfect color, but it's worth a try, because it is so simple. If you're happy with the color that results after reapplying the ink limit profile (and don't forget to Assign a Profile again, too), and the colors are below 240% in the *Info* panel, then go to "Create Your Cover PDF."

If you are not happy with the color after applying the 240% Ink Limit profile again, go to the *History* panel and go all the way back to the step before you applied the "HP Indigo" profile. (This will probably be labeled "Open.") Click there. Now your image has no profiles applied to it. It is just as it was when you first opened the file.

Now apply the color adjustments (in order) that you noted down earlier. (Remember, these adjustments made your cover look the way you wanted after the two profiles were applied.) Next, redo each step under the "Apply HP Indigo Profile to Cover" and then "Apply LSI Ink Limits to Cover" sections. Does the cover look the way you want it to now? Adjust the colors, always checking the ink percentages, until you find a solution that works for you!

## Method Three: If Only Bits of the Cover are Over 240%, Manually Adjust the Colors

Perhaps you've checked your cover, and only a few small portions of your image are over the required 240% ink limits. Should you apply either of the ICC profiles previously mentioned to your cover? Maybe not.

Instead, you could modify the troublesome color until it meets LSI's 240% ink percentage requirements. Go to *Select,* and then choose *Color Range.* Use the eyedropper to select the color you would like to modify. Adjust the settings so that you select all closely similar colors. Next, go to *Image, Adjustments,* and either choose "Hue/Saturation" (adjust the "Lightness" bar, and check the ink percentages in the Info box as you do so), or "Replace Color," and change the color to one you like, and one that meets LSI's ink percentage requirements. Both methods require a bit of experimenting. Good luck!

## Great Black Color 237% Ink Percentage

I'd be remiss if I didn't pass on to you the best secret I've found: How to make a perfect black color that passes LSI's stringent 240% ink saturation standards.

Please note that this great black color *only* works if you are working with CMYK color. Applying this black in RGB color mode will result in 300% ink saturation.

Please also note that this perfect black color can be used to adjust the black color of text and black shapes that you made in your original, layered CMYK cover. Apply the color to each individual, original layer. It does not work as well if you need to modify the black in a flat image, such as a photograph.

Use the settings on the next page to create a black that only registers at the 237% ink saturation level when it is applied within the CMYK color space.

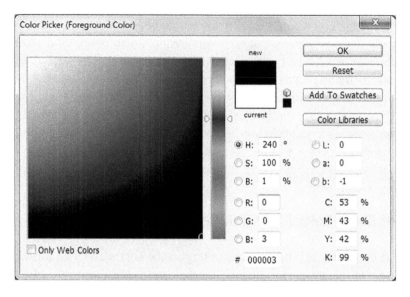

*CMYK Readout Settings*

- C: 53%
- M: 43%
- Y: 42%
- K: 99%

# Create Your Cover PDF

*Y*our cover image is finally ready. If you're working with the LSI template, open your template file once more. Make sure that the template file only consists of one layer—the template. If you previously placed your cover on the template, be sure to delete the layer containing the old version of your cover now.

For LSI covers, place your new cover image (*MyCoverCMYK2*) on the template, as detailed previously under the section entitled, "Lightning Source Cover Template," on page 158. Also, place your ISBN image (that you previously cropped and saved as a separate file) on the cover image, in a location that looks appropriate to you. The ISBN should be placed near the bottom of the back cover. Be certain it is well within the safety lines, so that it will print.

From now on all steps will apply to both LSI and CS templates (except the "Output Preview" section).

Flatten the image and choose the *File, Save As* function. Check the box next to "As a copy," and choose the file format "Photoshop PDF," as shown in the next image. Rename the file *ISBN_cov* (where ISBN is your book's actual ISBN, such as *9780984404445_cov*). This is the cover file name required by LSI. As far as I can tell, CS does not care what you name the file. However, it makes sense to name the file by the book's ISBN, so this file naming method works for both LSI and CS.

The next dialogue box (one may appear prior to this one, but just click *OK*), allows you to choose the PDF setting for your file. In the "Adobe PDF Preset" and "Standard" boxes choose PDF/X-1a:2001, if it is available in your version of Adobe Photoshop. Please see the following image for an example.

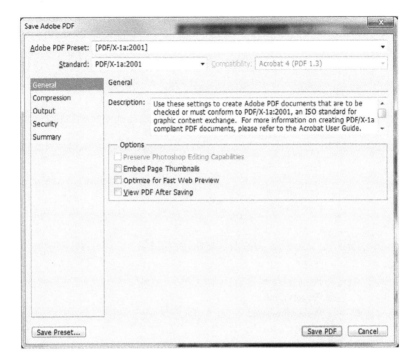

Then click "Save PDF." You are finished with this step.

*Tip for your PSD File:* In order to preserve your original, layered PSD cover file, in the *History* panel, now click the box immediately *before* the flatten image command. This will undo the flatten command. Save it. This way, you won't accidentally save your layered PSD file as a flat file.

## Output Preview (LSI Covers Only)

Next, open Adobe Acrobat Pro and open your new *ISBN_cov* PDF. It's time to check a few things in your file. The first will be those troublesome ink percentages. Go to *Advanced, Print Production,* and then click on "Output Preview." Check the box next to "Total Ink Coverage" and type "240" in the box. (Skip this step if you are working with a CreateSpace cover.)

In Adobe Acrobat X, go to *Tools, Print Production,* and then click on "Output Preview."

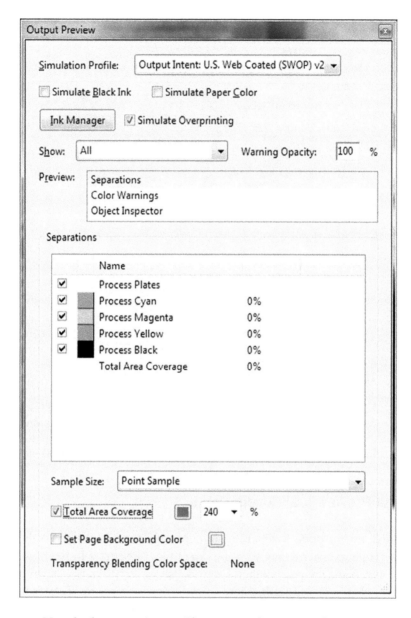

Now look at your image. If any areas show up with neon green speckles or blocks of neon green, you have trouble. While LSI may overlook very small areas that marginally go over the 240% ink limit, large areas may either get your file rejected, or LSI will "rasterize" it, which means that your image quality will downgrade. Your color may be affected, as well. Neither are good options. If you've carefully followed the instructions under "Adjust Cover Ink Percentages for LSI," this should not happen. If it does, go back through that section again.

> *Note:* You may wish to check your *MyCoverCMYK2* cover file in *Output Preview* before you go to the trouble of placing it on the template. I often do, just so I don't have to repeat steps if the ink saturation levels are a little off. Simply flatten your *MyCoverCMYK* file, and save as a PDF or TIFF file. Check the resulting file in *Output Preview* in Adobe Acrobat.

## Save Cover as a PostScript File

You've almost finished processing your cover file! It's been a long road, but it will be a wonderful achievement when you are finished, and have a perfect file ready to upload to LSI or CS.

Save the file as a PostScript file (.ps) in Adobe Acrobat. Go to *File,* and choose *Save As.* Leave the file name the same, and hit the arrow down button next to "save as type." Choose the PostScript ".ps" extension and save.

Close the PDF file that you have open (or you will get an error message with the next step), but leave the Adobe Acrobat program open.

Next, go back to *Advanced, Print Production,* and this time choose "Acrobat Distiller." Make sure PDF/X-1a:2001 is selected in the "Default Settings." If not, click the arrow down button and select it.

> As mentioned in the previous section, in Adobe Acrobat X, go to *Tools, Print Production,* and then click on "Acrobat Distiller."

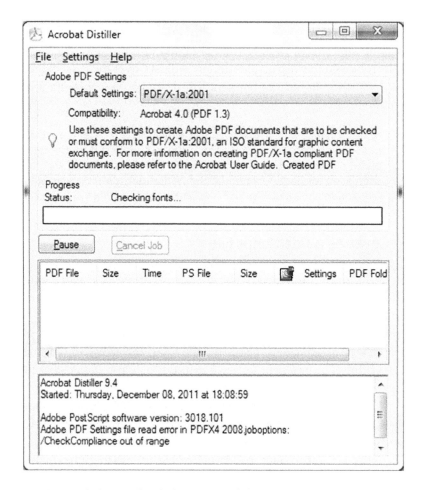

Next, click on *File*, click *Open*, and find the PostScript ".ps" file you just saved. Click on it, and then click *Open*. Acrobat Distiller will now process the file so it will meet all PDF/X-1a:2001 specifications. Distiller saves the file as a PDF file, and, if you left the ".ps" file name the same as your original PDF file name, it will replace your original PDF file.

## Check File Properties

You can now open the new PDF file in Adobe Acrobat again, and check the settings under *File,* and then *Properties.* Check on the

"Description" tab and check at the bottom of the dialogue box to make sure it was processed by Acrobat Distiller (of course, it was). Then check the "Custom" tab. It should state "PDF/X-1a:2001" in the "Value" box. See the next image.

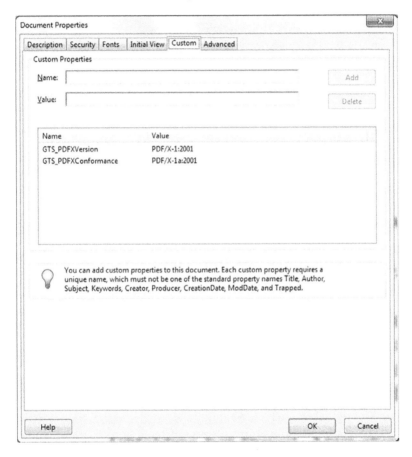

Last of all, I like to check the image dpi of the document one final time. This is not strictly necessary, but I prefer to make sure my file is completely compliant to LSI standards before I send it off.

To check, go to *Advanced, Print Production,* and choose "Pre-flight." Click on the custom profile you made earlier, named "Images Greater than 0 dpi." Instructions for making a custom profile can be found in the section entitled, "Set Up a Custom Profile in Preflight," located on page 95, in *Part One* of this book. After the file has run through Acrobat Distiller, the image dpi will be a hair less than 300 dpi. That is okay. See the following image for an example.

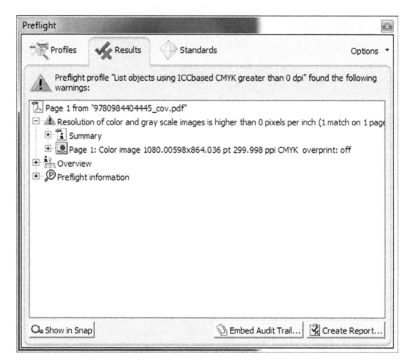

Your file is finished! Now you can send your *ISBN_cov* file and *ISBN_txt* files to LSI (or CS).

As a fellow author and publisher, I know first-hand that writing and/or publishing a book is a long, hard road. You can be proud that you accomplished each step along the way.

Soon you will hold your very own printed book in your hands. Let me just say, there is nothing like it. That moment makes all of this work worthwhile.

Congratulations, and I wish you many book sales!

# To Do List for Processing a Cover File

1. Save cover image as a new name
2. Make sure the images in your cover are 300 dpi
3. Download the cover template from LSI or CS
4. Crop out the ISBN for an LSI template; save it as a separate file
5. Flatten the cover template
6. Place your cover on the template, and ensure that it is the right size; if not, adjust it separately. (Those with CreateSpace covers can then place it on the template again, after it is adjusted.)
7. Make sure that all of your text and important images fall within the template's safety lines. Remember that the outer edges of your book will be trimmed away when the book is manufactured. Account for this when you create your cover; position elements accordingly, so they will look "balanced" on the page between the safety guide lines.
8. Convert your cover to CMYK color (convert template and cover for CS; cover file only for LSI)
9. (LSI covers only) Convert cover image ink percentages to 240% ink limits (maximum saturation)
10. (LSI cover only) place cover image that has been adjusted to 240% ink limits onto the template. Place the ISBN on the template, as well
11. Create your cover pdf
12. (LSI covers only) Check your ink percentages in Adobe Acrobat's *Output Preview*

13. Save the PDF as a PostScript file, and then process the PostScript file through Acrobat Distiller, using the PDF/X-1a:2001 setting
14. Check your file's properties, using the *File, Properties* dialogue box

# Amazon's "Look Inside the Book" Program

## Look Inside the Book

*I*f you have a seller account on Amazon (or sign up for one), you may like to include your print book in Amazon's "Look Inside the Book" (LITB) program. This program allows customers to read a sample of your print book online.

If your book is uploaded to Kindle, your potential readers already have the opportunity to download a sample of your ebook. However, many people interested in buying print copies of your book may not know that the Kindle download sample is available for viewing on their PC or other viewing device. In addition, the formatting for the Kindle edition is very different than for the print edition, as we have already established. Fancy title fonts, headers, eye-pleasing spacing, etc., are probably not available in your Kindle edition. LITB allows you to show your readers the beauty of your print book, as well as to read a sample of your book. It can be a great selling opportunity for your print editions.

One thing to note when you enter your book into the LITB program is that your cover image in Amazon's search results and on its detail page will be altered. It will have "Look Inside!" text positioned just above and partially wrapped around the top portion of your cover graphic. As a result, your thumbnail cover image on Amazon is reduced in size. This smaller image size may diminish your cover's visual appeal to potential customers. On the other hand, it may enhance interest, for the readers will know they can sample the inside of the book and see if they like your writing style.

General information about the "Look Inside the Book" program can be found on Amazon's website:

*http://www.amazon.com/gp/help/customer/display.html?nodeId=1 3685751*

The webpage accessed by the previous link provides all of the basic details you will need in order to learn more about the program. I won't cover those issues here. Instead, I will focus upon showing you how to prepare your document for Amazon's LITB program. Specifically, we'll go through its *Option One* requirements.

## Sign Up for the "Look Inside the Book" Program

In order to participate in the "Look Inside the Book" program, you will first need an Amazon seller account. If you do not have one, now is the time to set one up. Amazon's "Seller Central" (and registration) can be found at the following link:

*http://sellercentral.amazon.com*

You can sign-up for a "Look Inside the Book" upload account by sending an email request to:

*insidethebook-submission@amazon.com.*

Amazon will then add that functionality to your seller page.

Once you have registered for the LITB program, your seller account page will show a file upload link for "Search Inside the Book" (now known as LITB) on the left side of the screen. Click on the *PDF & Cover Upload* link to upload your book.

## Prepare Your Images for LITB

Amazon requires that your images be 300 dpi, so you will use your cover file to make the cover image required for LITB.

Open your final PSD cover file, and save it under a new name. (I also like to save all of my Amazon LITB files in a folder named *Amazon_LITB*, just to keep the files clearly labeled and separated from the originals).

Flatten it and crop it in order to remove the LSI/CS template. I like to zoom in to about 200% to make sure that only the image is selected before I crop it (and that no parts of the template remain in the selected image). This will give a cleaner cover image to upload to Amazon.

If your file is in CMYK color, convert it to RGB color by going to *Edit,* and then *Convert to Profile.* Choose RGB profile "sRGB IEC61966-2.1," which, according to digital color space professionals, produces the best RGB color. Click *OK.* Next, go to *Edit, Assign Profile,* and make sure the same RGB file format (sRGB IEC61966-2.1) is selected. Click *OK.*

Save the file.

Your next steps will be to crop out the front cover, back cover, and spine, using Adobe Photoshop's crop tool. Crop each image separately, and save it "as a copy," and as a different name (such as Front_Cover). Save as either a TIFF or JPG. Once one file is cropped, step backward (undo) the last action. This may be accomplished by going to the *History* panel and clicking on the step prior to the crop. Now the cover should be whole once more, and you can crop your next image from the cover file.

Once you have created your three separate image files, you are ready to move on to the next step.

## Prepare your Print Microsoft Word .doc for LITB

Open your *print* book Microsoft Word document. (Not your ebook document.)

Amazon requires that LITB PDF files be named by your book's ISBN. (No dashes.) For example, your PDF file might be named *0123456789.pdf* (do not include ".pdf" in the file name, for Adobe Acrobat will automatically add the .pdf extension when it makes the file).

In order to preserve your original print document, save your LITB print document as the new ISBN name, and save it in your new Amazon LITB folder.

Turn on the "Show/Hide" formatting marks.

Go to the *very* beginning of your document and insert a "next page" section break. Put your cursor just before the section break and hit "return" to add an extra paragraph space.

Insert your front cover image. You may need to hit "return" again after the image, if it does not show up. (If your image still does not display correctly, see the tip at the end of this section.)

Next, click on the image. Check its paragraph formatting to make sure it is centered, and also check the ruler bar to make certain its position is not indented. If it is indented, move the "first line indent" triangle on the ruler so that it is flush with the left margin.

Go to the very end of your book and insert a "next page" break. Insert the back cover after the section break. Repeat the procedure to insert your spine image. Save the file.

Print the Microsoft Word .doc to PDF, being sure to select the correct trim size for your book, and also select the PDF/X-1a:2001 setting.

> *Tip:* If your image does not show up after you've inserted it in your document, or if it only shows the bottom sliver of the picture, check the following settings in your Microsoft Word document:
>
> - Hit "return" after the image, and see if it shows up.
> - If not, make sure that "exact" line spacing for that page is turned off. Here's how to do it: Select the image and any paragraph returns within that single page. Go to your *Paragraph* dialogue box and click on the "Indents and Spacing" tab. Under the "Indentation" section, make sure that the line spacing is set at "single," not "exactly."
> - If that does not work, in Microsoft Word 2003, go to *Tools, Options,* and under the "View" tab make sure that the "Picture placeholders" box is deselected (in 2010 it is located under *File, Options, Advanced,* "Show document content," and then "Show picture placeholders"). In addition, make sure that the "Drawings" box is selected (in 2010 it is named "Show drawings and text boxes...," and it is located directly beneath "Show picture placeholders").

## Create Bookmarks in Your LITB PDF

Amazon requests that bookmarks be made for the different sections of your book. The minimum bookmarks required are for the front cover and for the start of the body text (Chapter One, for example). Amazon also would like the back cover and spine bookmarked, if they are included.

Amazon used to have a handy table detailing exactly what they would like bookmarked in the file, and how they would like it named. I can no longer find that file on their website, although I do still have the original table. While I assume (since it is no longer available), that the information is now obsolete, I continue to use the table as a guideline. You might wish to, as well. Here it is:

| Bookmark | Required Component? | Description |
|---|---|---|
| Front Cover | Yes | The front cover of the book. |
| Front Flap | No | The front flap of the dust jacket, if available. |
| Copyright | No | The copyright page of the book. |
| Table of Contents | No | The first page of the table of contents. |
| Front Matter | No | Front matter includes the title page, preface, introduction, dedication, etc. If the front matter is not contiguous, use one bookmark for each section of Front Matter content. |
| Body | Yes | Bookmark for the first page of the text, i.e. Chapter 1. |
| Index | No | The first page of the index. |
| Back Matter | No | Back matter includes the bibliography, afterword, epilogue, etc. If the back matter is not contiguous, use one bookmark for each section of Back Matter content. |
| Back Flap | No | The back flap of the dusk jacket, if available. |
| Back Cover | No | |
| Spine | No | |

Determine which bookmarks you would like to insert. Next, we'll learn the simple process of inserting bookmarks into your PDF file.

The following page shows an example of bookmarks that were made for a Civil War book published by Diamond Press.

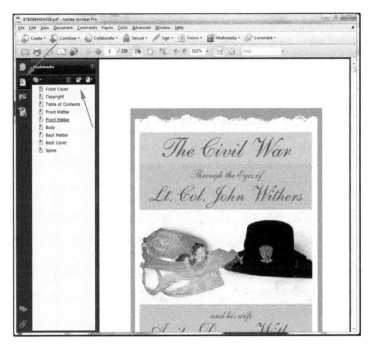

*Previous Image Enlarged*

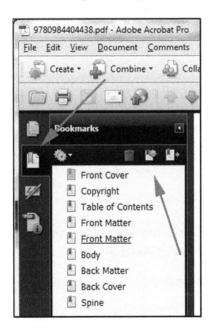

Bookmarks are easy to make in Adobe Acrobat Pro. Simply click the "Bookmarks" icon and the bookmarks panel will open. (In the preceding picture, the arrow in the left margin points to the "Bookmarks" icon.) To add a bookmark, click in your document in the exact place where you would like to place a bookmark. For example, click at the top of your front cover image. Click the "Add a Bookmark" icon (the second arrow points to this button). Name it "Front Cover" (without quotes). Next, click the white space below the bookmark you just added, so you don't accidentally delete it when you add a new bookmark.

Go the next point in your document where you would like to place a bookmark, click there, and then click the "Add a Bookmark" icon and type in your new bookmark. Repeat the procedure until you have added all the bookmarks desired to your document.

Click on each of your bookmarks to make sure they take you to the correct bookmarked spot in your manuscript.

Save your PDF.

## Upload Your PDF to LITB

Now you're ready to upload your book to Amazon's "Look Inside the Book" program. Go to your seller account on Amazon.

*http://sellercentral.amazon.com*

Once you're in your account, take a look at the box on the left side of your screen. "Search Inside the Book" (now known as "Look Inside the Book") is listed, along with a link to upload your new LITB file. Click on the link entitled, "PDF & Cover Upload," and upload your file.

## Remove Your Book from LITB

If you join the LITB program, and later would like your book(s) removed, you may contact Amazon directly at:

*insidethebook-submission@amazon.com*

If you encounter difficulties in removing your book from the LITB program, please visit the following link for additional help:

*http://www.asiteaboutnothing.net/w_opt-out-of-look-inside.html*

# Appendix A

## Convert Microsoft Word Documents to PDF, Using Adobe Acrobat Program

Sometimes the print to Adobe PDF function may not work correctly in the Microsoft Word program. If this is the case, an alternate method of creating the PDF/X-1a:2001 file for your LSI or CS file is available.

Open Adobe Acrobat. In the *Open* dialogue box, under "Files of type," click the down arrow so that it shows "All files." Open your Microsoft Word .doc for your print book.

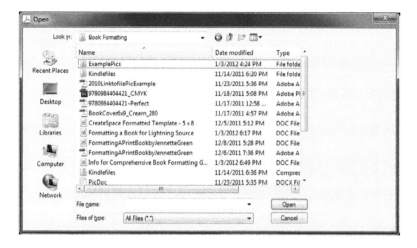

Save it as a PDF—be sure to name it *ISBN_txt,* as mentioned earlier in the book.

Go to *File,* then *Properties* and under the "Description" tab, make sure that the "PDF Producer" is Acrobat Distiller. (If not, go to the section entitled, "Save Your PDF as an Adobe PostScript File," which is located on page 93.) Also, while you're still in the "Description" tab, check to make sure that the "Page size" is the correct trim size for your book. It should be, but if it is not, you will need to crop it. (Go to *Document,* and then "Crop Pages." If you've made changes, save the file again.)

If you have images in the file, go to the "Color vs. Grayscale Images in Book Interior" section on page 90, and follow the steps listed.

# Appendix *B*

# Troubleshooting eBooks

Sometimes trouble arises with an ebook—especially with Smashwords' "Meatgrinder." Problems can arise with Kindle, as well. A common factor that creates many problems is when the document contains too many styles (such as Normal vs. Body styles). The styles may conflict with one another, or cause additional problems, which may raise a red flag at Smashwords or Kindle. If this happens, you have several options. First of all, go through the "Format eBooks" part of this book again, and make certain that you have followed *all* of the instructions. If that does not solve the problem, try one of the following solutions:

## Reformat the Document – Two Methods

### Method One: Apply Times New Roman and Single Spacing

Select the entire document (press the two keys "Ctrl + A"), and choose Times New Roman font, 12 pt.

While the entire document is still selected, go to *Format, Paragraph,* and make sure that the "Line spacing" is set to "single."

After you have done this, you will need to go through your document and reformat your title and chapter title headings so that they are a little larger (if you like) than the body text, but still within Smashwords' maximum point recommendations (14 pt.).

Check through your document and make sure everything is as you'd like it to be, and then re-upload to Smashwords.

### Method Two: Nuclear Purge

If the previous step does not take care of the issue (and you've also checked for "hidden bookmarks," which is explained in the following section), you may need to do a "nuclear purge" of your entire document. Only do this method as a last resort, because it will eliminate *all* of your formatting, including italics, bold, etc.

Select the entire document "Ctrl + A" and then in *the Styles and Formatting* panel click on "Clear Formatting." Alternately, for a more complete "purge," copy all of your text and paste it into a text editor, such as Notepad. Then copy all of the text in Notepad and paste it in an empty Word document.

After you've eliminated all of the formatting in your document, you will need to go back through your entire document and add back your first line indents (if used), reformat your chapter title headings, numbered lists, etc., in the appropriate point sizes accepted by Smashwords. You will also need to reapply italics, bold, and other formatting to your document.

The "nuclear purge" step is drastic, so don't do it unless you're desperate!

## Eliminate Hidden Bookmarks

"Hidden bookmarks" can also cause problems for Smashwords' "Meatgrinder." If you've added bookmarks and hyperlinks to your Table of Contents, check for the hidden bookmarks that Microsoft Word may have added, and delete them. This is easy enough to do.

Go to *Insert, Bookmark,* and check the box by "Hidden bookmarks." Then highlight each hidden bookmark in the box and delete it. Be certain not to delete the bookmarks that *you* placed in your document! Hidden bookmarks will have names similar to those in the following image.

# Appendix C

## Advanced eBook Formatting

### ePub Files

At the time of this book's publication, the main distributor which absolutely requires an .ePub file is Apple, although many ebook distributors will accept .ePub files, right along with other ebook file formats. If you choose to distribute to Apple through LSI, you will need to provide LSI with an .ePub file that will pass the .ePub Validator file check, found at the site listed after this paragraph. This is also true if you decide to form an account with Apple and upload the file directly to their site.

**ePub Validator**
*http://validator.idpf.org*

Smashwords' "Meatgrinder" creates an .ePub file of your book that the company will submit to Apple if your book is included in the Smashwords Premium Catalog. If you use Smashwords, you will not need to create your own .ePub file. However, do not take the file that Smashwords created and then upload it yourself to iBookstore, or to another retailer. This violates the Smashwords Terms of Service agreement.

*https://www.smashwords.com/about/tos*

Other methods to create an .ePub file include:

### Jutoh or eCub

Jutoh or eCub (a free version of Jutoh) are programs which can create an .ePub file.

*http://www.jutoh.com/*

*http://www.juliansmart.com/ecub*

### Lulu's Free .ePub Converter

Lulu now provides a free .ePub converter service that can convert your Microsoft Word .doc, .docx, and .rtf files into the .ePub format. Be certain to read their documentation before uploading your file. However, if you followed the advice in this book as you prepared your print and ebook documents, very few items will need to be adjusted in your file for Lulu's converter. For more information, read their Creator Guide.

**ePub Converter Main Page**
*http://www.lulu.com/publish/ebooks/*

**ePub eBook Creator Guide**
*http://connect.lulu.com/t5/eBook-Formatting-Publishing/eBook-Creator-Guide/ta-p/109443*

## Calibre

Calibre is a wonderful, free program that can create a multitude of ebook format files. However, at the time of this book's publication, their .ePub files do not pass the ePub Validator  listed at the beginning of this Appendix.

Calibre's website:
*http://calibre-ebook.com/*

## Kindle NCX files

Do you have a nonfiction book with a number of important chapters that your readers might like to access without having to return to the Table of Contents? Kindle provides the NCX view, which provides a list of all the chapters in the book. The person reading the book can be at any location in the book, click the NCX view, and see a listing of all of your book's chapters and sections. He can then click on one of the sections to go directly to that place in your document. This format is very handy for nonfiction with a lot of different sections.

How to make a NCX file? Here is one place to find help with formatting NCX and other files for KF8 (Kindle Advanced Formatting). This link is one page in a series of posts on the overall subject:

*http://www.helenhanson.com/?p=1227*

## Links for Kindle and PubIt! Advanced Formatting

Kindle—Reduce book content file size (if images make it too large):
*https://kdp.amazon.com/self-publishing/help?topicId=AQY9VBML4LKPK*

Kindle—Advanced formatting (Amazon Kindle formatting guidelines):
*http://kindlegen.s3.amazonaws.com/AmazonKindlePublishingGuidelines.pdf*

Barnes & Noble's PubIt! ePub Formatting Guide for NOOK:
*https://simg1.imagesbn.com/pimages/pubit/support/pubit_epub_formatting_guide.pdf*

# Appendix *D*

## Build Your Cover Image on the Cover Template

This section is for book covers that, for one reason or another, need to be reconstructed or cropped. First, make sure that you have read the following chapters, which are located within *Part Three* of this book:

- Cover Resolution, page 146
- The Cover Template, page 149
- Place Your Cover Image on the Template, page 165

Next, open the LSI or CS template that you will need for your book cover.

## CreateSpace Covers

For the CS template, drag guides to delineate the safety zone for the spine, the ISBN bar code space (if you want CreateSpace to place the ISBN bar code for you), and the inner peach safety zones. In the image below, the black guide lines appear to extend off of the page.

### CS Template

If you are working with a CS cover, please go to page 213, to the section entitled, "Building a Cover on the Template." Now you can build directly on your template.

## Lightning Source Covers

Drag guide lines onto the template corresponding to each of the blue safety bars . It is vital to know the exact location of each safety line. This way, you can ensure that important text and images are safely placed inside these lines. If spine text, or front or back cover text crosses over the safety lines, your file will be rejected.

In the following picture, the black guide lines appear to extend off of the page.

## *LSI Template*

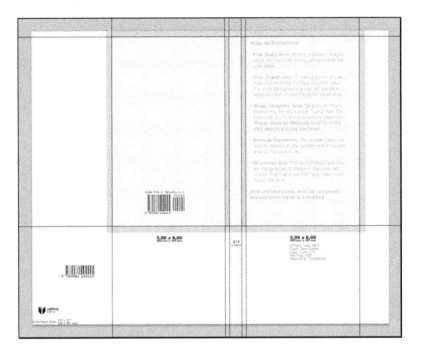

The next step will be to mark off the actual cover area of the template and crop it out. The cover will be built on this cropped layer.

Why crop out the cover region on the LSI template? Why not build on the original template? Here is why: We'll later be modifying the cover's ink percentages (CS covers do not need this adjustment). If the cover was built on the original template, the template would be modified, as well. I prefer to keep the original PSD template exactly as it arrived from LSI. Crop marks will remain the 100% registration black, etc. The cover will be placed on the template after it has been fully processed for LSI.

Drag guides to the outer edge of the blue bars located on the four outermost edges of the cover area, and then crop the template.

Rename the file. I rename my file *MyCoverCMYK*. The arrows in the bottom left corner of the following two images show where to place the guide lines, relative to the blue bars, to crop the image. Place guide lines on all four sides of the template, following the example shown in the last picture on this page.

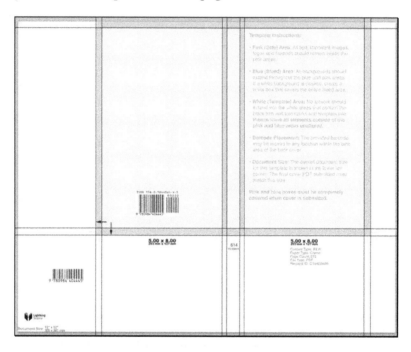

*Close Up of Guide Placement*

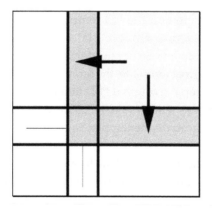

## Template About to be Cropped

After you have cropped the template and saved it as a new name, you will start to build your cover.

## Building a Cover on the Template

If you are building a cover for LSI, you may want to choose colors that adhere to LSI's 240% ink saturation limit. If you need a good black color that will fit these standards, see "Great Black Ink 237% Saturation," at the end of this Appendix. This great black color will only work when applied in CMYK color mode.

I like to build my covers in CMYK color mode. That way, I have no surprises. My CMYK colors print just like I expect. On the other hand, if I build my cover in RGB color, I may be disappointed by how some of the bright RGB colors convert to CMYK colors (this has happened on several occasions). Other publishers prefer to work with RGB color. The choice is yours.

Make certain the images you place on your cover are 300 dpi. Keep your important text and images within the safety lines. Also make sure that all of your text and important images fall within the template's safety lines. Remember that the outer edges of your book will be trimmed away when the book is manufactured. Account for this when creating your cover, and when positioning your text and images on the template. Use the vertical and horizontal safety lines as your guides to keep your cover elements balanced, and positioned correctly on the page.

With CreateSpace covers, make certain that your cover image completely extends to the outside edge of the thick peach outer lines—but please do not let your cover extend beyond these markings. When you are finished, either turn off the guide layer, or make sure that your cover image completely conceals it, or the cover may be rejected. Flatten the cover and template. Save it as a new name.

When you are finished with the LSI cover, flatten it and save it as a new name (perhaps *MyCoverCMYK,* as mentioned earlier in this book).

## Cropping a Cover on the Template

If your LSI cover only needs to be cropped so that it will fit on the template, place the cover on the cropped template you just made in the "Lightning Source Covers" section of this Appendix. Crop the cover image so that it fits correctly. Flatten the image. You may wish to name your new cover file exactly as you did earlier (*My-CoverCMYK*)).

If your CreateSpace template merely needs to be trimmed, crop it so that it fits the template. Then place it on the original template once more.

## Final Steps

When you are finished with the preceding steps, you will need to go to the chapter entitled, "Convert Your Cover to CMYK Color," which is located on page 167, within *Part Three* of this book. Open your new flattened cover (for CS, use the flattened cover/template file; for LSI, use the flattened cover only), and then follow the steps provided. LSI covers will then need to be converted to 240% ink limits. Follow the instructions provided (in order) in the earlier sections of this book.

> *Note:* If you do not have Adobe Photoshop, and if you have created a CreateSpace cover file in another image program, be sure to save it as a TIFF file. Flatten it. Then open your flattened TIFF file in Adobe Acrobat. Next, go to the section entitled, "Save Cover as a PostScript File," which is located on page 187, at the end of *Part Three*. Follow the instructions from there on.

## Great Black, 237% Ink Saturation

Please note that this great black color *only* works if you are working in the CMYK color space. Applying this black in RGB color mode will result in 300% ink saturation.

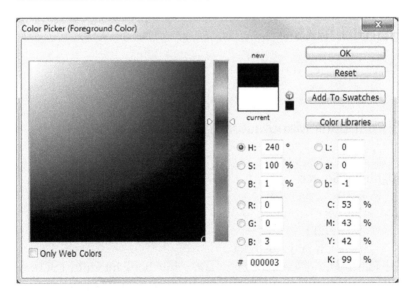

*CMYK Readout Settings*

- C: 53%
- M: 43%
- Y: 42%
- K: 99%

# Appendix *E*

## Helpful Links

### POD Print Book Manufacturing/Distribution

#### Lightning Source

LSI—Can set discount as low as:
   20% in U.S.
   25% in UK and Australia
Besides offering standard black and white book interiors, LSI now offers Standard Color for POD, which utilizes new inkjet technology. LSI also continues to offer Premium Color, which costs a little more per page than the Standard Color option. See your US POD Agreement and Operating Manual for details.

*http://www.lightningsource.com*

### Amazon's CreateSpace

*https://www.createspace.com/Products/Book*

# eBook Distribution Sites

### Amazon's Kindle Direct Publishing (KDP)

*Accepted file formats:*
1. html (made from a Microsoft Word .doc file). A zip file is needed if images are included in the document.
2. .ePub

*Max file size:* 50 megabytes
*Cover Image upload size:* Minimum of 1000 pixels on the longest side (in height); however, 2500 pixels on longest side is preferred. JPG or TIFF format, in RGB color space. Ideal height/width ratio: 1.6. (Height 1.6 times greater than the width.)

Here is Kindle's Faq for more information:

*https://kdp.amazon.com/self-publishing/help?topicId=A2J0TRG6OPX0VM*

*Maximum Kindle screen size for images:* 600 x 800 pixels
*http://kdp.amazon.com/*

*Royalties*: If your ebook is priced between $2.99 and $9.99, you can select the 70% royalty option.  By choosing this option, you will receive 70% of the ebook's list price. If your ebook is priced lower or higher than those limits, you must select the 35% royalty option.

### Barnes & Noble's PubIt!

*Accepted file formats:*
1. .ePub
2. Microsoft Word .doc, .docx file
3. rtf file

4.  html (zipped file, if book includes images)
5.  txt file

*Max file size:* 20 megabytes
*Cover Image upload size:* Minimum of 1200 pixels on the longest side; however, 2000 pixels on longest side is recommended.
*NOOK screen size for images:* 600 x 730 pixels

*http://pubit.barnesandnoble.com/*


### Smashwords

*Accepted file format*: Microsoft Word .doc file
*Max file size:* 5 megabytes
*Cover Image upload size:* Minimum of 1400 pixels *wide.*
*http://blog.smashwords.com/2012/06/new-ebook-cover-image-requirements.html*
*Distribution:* Your ebook must qualify for inclusion in their Premium Catalog before it will distributed to these sales channels:
1.  Sony
2.  Barnes & Noble
3.  Kobo
4.  Apple iBookstore
5.  Diesel eBooks
6.  Amazon (deselect this option if you upload to KDP directly)

*http://www.smashwords.com/*

Smashwords Style Guide:
*http://www.smashwords.com/books/view/52*


### Lightning Source: Standard LSI eBook Program

*Accepted file formats:*
1.  PDF
2.  .ePub
3.  .pdb

*Description:* LSI accepts html tags in the book description (annotation) field.

*Marketing Image:* 510 x 680 pixels, 96 dpi, JPG format, RGB color.

*Discount*: Can set as low as 25%. If you would like to set it lower, please contact your LSI ebook representative for more information.

*Distribution:* The main retail partners to whom the Standard LSI eBook Program distributes are:
1. BooksOnBoard
2. Powells
3. Diesel eBooks
4. eBookMall

Please note that this list is *not* inclusive. The LSI Standard eBook Program distributes ebooks to a large number of other sites, as well. However, not every ebook retailer will list every book in LSI's catalog feed. In other words, your book is not guaranteed to be carried by those additional sites. Contact your LSI ebook representative for a complete retailer list.

## Lightning Source: Independent Publishers Program (IPP)

This LSI ebook distribution program provides publishers with access to additional online retailers. For more details, see the section in this book entitled, "Independent Publisher Program (IPP), located near the end of *Part Two* in this book. Your LSI sales representative can provide additional information.

As a part of this program LSI can distribute your book to Barnes & Noble and Amazon (Amazon requires signing a separate agreement; carefully read this for their discount terms—it may be more beneficial to upload directly to Amazon).

Apple iBookstore (requires a separate agreement, and .ePub upload; compare this agreement with Smashwords to see which program would be most beneficial for your book's profitability; also carefully read for any exclusivity clauses.)

*http://www.lightningsource.com*

### OmniLit/All Romance eBooks
*http://www.omnilit.com/*

### Google eBooks
*http://support.google.com/books/partner/*

### BookStrand
*http://www.bookstrand.com/*

### Trapezium eBooks
*http://www.trapeziumebooks.com/*

## Books in Print, ISBN, PCN Program, and more...

### Books in Print
If you own your own ISBN(s), you will want to make sure that *Books in Print* has all of the information on your book. You can create a title record at either *MyIdentifiers,* or *BowkerLINK*. Here are the respective links:

### MyIdentifiers
*https://www.myidentifiers.com/*

### BowkerLINK
*http://www.bowkerlink.com/corrections/common/home.asp*

### Nielsen PubWeb

*www.nielsenbookdata.com/pubweb*

Nielsen PubWeb provides book information for books in the United Kingdom. It is an online electronic title record editing service. If you request a publisher's account, you can upload this information manually. To open an account, click on the "Not a registered User?" link, fill out the document, and email it to PubWeb, as described in the instructions.

When you create a title record for your book at Nielsen PubWeb, you will need to enter categories for your book. A link to find the BIC codes is available on the site. It also can be found here:

*http://editeur.dyndns.org/bic_categories*

The main BIC Basic website page can be found here:
*http://www.bic.org.uk/17/BIC-Basic/*

## iPage

Lightning Source updates information to iPage, but you might want to check and see that everything is correct. Ask your LSI representative to set up an account for you; you can check your book's metadata and cover here:

*https://ipage.ingrambook.com*

## BISAC Subject Headings

These subject headings are used when entering your book title information at LSI. I've found it makes things simpler if I decide upon these categories before uploading to LSI. Find them here:

*http://www.bisg.org/what-we-do-0-136-bisac-subject-headings-list-major-subjects.php*

## Library of Congress Preassigned Control Number (PCN) program

Be certain to mail the PCN program a print copy of your book soon after publication; read all of their requirements carefully on the website.

*http://www.loc.gov/publish/pcn/*

**Library of Congress Subject Headings can be found at either of the following sites:**

*http://www.melvyl.worldcat.org/*

*http://www.worldcat.org/*

When you enter the WorldCat site and enter a search term, it may ask you to continue as a guest. Click on that button to continue.

Search for books similar to yours, and then check in the *Subjects* section on the right side of the book's detail page. Click on the "View all subjects" link, and it will take you to the bottom of the book detail page for more ideas. This is a great research site for this purpose. If you sign up with the PCN program, you can print both the PCN number and the Library of Congress Subject headings on the copyright page of your book. These classifications help librarians to better classify your book.

# Miscellaneous Helpful Sites

## Yahoo Groups for POD and Self-Publishers

### Print on Demand Publishers
*http://finance.groups.yahoo.com/group/pod_publishers/*

### Self-Publishing: Publishing Discussions and Answers
*http://finance.groups.yahoo.com/group/Self-Publishing/*

## Reducing Your eBook's File Size

For tips on reducing the file size of your ebook, visit Kindle's FAQ, entitled, "Reducing Your Book Content File Size." It is located at the following link:

*https://kdp.amazon.com/self-publishing/
help?topicId=AQY9VBML4LKPK*

## Create Book Covers Using Scribus

John Cullerton has written an ebook entitled, *Create Book Covers with Scribus*. It can be purchased here:

*http://www.booklocker.com/books/4055.html*

## Article on Amazon's Expanded Distribution Channel

Aaron Shepard has written a comprehensive article about Amazon's EDC program. It can be found here:

*http://www.newselfpublishing.com/CreateSpaceEDC.html*

## ISBN Bar Codes

Crop from Lightning Source template.
Or try the following links:

*http://www.terryburton.co.uk/barcodewriter/generator/*

*http://www.tux.org/~milgram/bookland/indexUsual.html*

## Format a Book Website and Forum

If you have questions, comments, or feedback, please stop by our new help forum and let us know!

*www.formatabook.com*

For updates, visit:

*http://www.formatabook.com/updates/*

# Author's Note

*I*t is my great hope that *Book Formatting for Self-Publishers, A Comprehensive How-To Guide* has been of benefit to you. I remember how overwhelmed I felt when I first started out in the publishing field several years ago. All of the new technical details of publishing seemed unending. As well, it took quite a bit of trial and error to learn how to produce files that work well for the different print and ebook formats. My hope is that this book will help you learn the process in a much faster way, using simple, step-by-step instructions.

You've learned that you really can produce a professionally formatted book by using Microsoft Word and Adobe Acrobat. Even better, you can compete on a level playing field with the publishing giants at online retail outlets, such as Amazon.com. The possibilities are limitless, with a great book and a well thought out marketing plan.

If you've found this book helpful, please consider writing a positive review on Amazon—it would be very much appreciated! It also will help others find this book.

If you have questions, comments, or if you find broken links, please visit the new *Help Forum* at *www.formatabook.com*, and let us know. It is my goal to keep this book current, and its information as complete as possible. Also, visit the *Updates* page for new updates.

The stigma of self-publishing is vanishing. Now is the time for talented authors and publishers to make their mark in this fast-changing industry.

I wish you the very best, and many, many book sales!

Jennette Green
*www.formatabook.com*
*www.diamondpresspublishing.com*
*www.jennettegreen.com*

# $\mathcal{I}$ndex

Printed in Australia
AUHW011852200220
324037AU00049B/331